The Royal Commission on Historical Manuscripts

Guides to Sources for British History
based on the National Register of Archives

3

GUIDE TO THE LOCATION OF COLLECTIONS
Described in the Reports and Calendars Series 1870 – 1980

London   Her Majesty's Stationery Office

HER MAJESTY'S STATIONERY OFFICE

Government Bookshops

49 High Holborn, London WC1V 6HB
13a Castle Street, Edinburgh EH2 3AR
41 The Hayes, Cardiff CF1 1JW
Brazennose Street, Manchester M60 8AS
Southey House, Wine Street, Bristol BS1 2BQ
258 Broad Street Birmingham B1 2HE
80 Chichester Street, Belfast BT1 4JY

*Government Publications are also available
through booksellers*

ISBN 0 11 440144 6

Preface

The 236 volumes of Reports and Calendars which the Commission has published since 1869 describe a total of 624 privately owned collections of historical papers. At the date of their examination 410 of these were in the possession of families or private individuals and 214 in that of corporate and other institutions.

The scope and detail of the accounts published of each collection varied considerably. Many of those opened to the Commission's earliest exploratory inspections were found to contain very little material of historical substance. In some cases only a few selected documents were produced for its examination and while these were described at length, the larger collections from which they came were necessarily passed by in silence. The range of what might be described was in all cases limited by the Commission's undertaking to owners to ignore anything of a private or personal nature. This led in practice to the exclusion of virtually all papers later in date than 1800 and large numbers of earlier accumulations of deeds of title and estate papers. Perhaps most seriously, the Commission was also prevented by lack of resources, especially after 1914, from preparing as many detailed calendars of major collections as had originally been planned.

But if, for all these reasons, the collective scale and contents of the reports may now seem uneven, relatively little in private hands that was of importance for national history before 1800 in fact escaped their notice completely. Despite their shortcomings, they have consequently remained a major and much used repertorium for research.

Since the reports were compiled, however, many of the collections they describe have been moved, and in some cases altogether dispersed, so that scholars have found their present whereabouts increasingly difficult to trace. The Commission has already made three attempts to deal with this problem by including revised location lists in its 22nd, 24th and 25th *Reports to the Crown*, published in 1946, 1962 and 1967. But as the research on which these were based had often to be limited to enquiries addressed to the original owners or their successors, their shortcomings have long been apparent.

The present Guide has consequently been undertaken as an entirely fresh piece of research, and has drawn upon a much more comprehensive range of sources, including most notably the large amounts of unpublished information that have now been brought together in the National Register of Archives. While it cannot attempt to record the whereabouts of every individual document mentioned in each report it is hoped that it may at least have succeeded in indicating that of every major item or group and also, where relevant, that of other connected groups which the reports themselves may have left unnoticed. In cases of loss or disappearance, the point at which this occurred has been identified whenever possible.

In its performance of these tasks the Guide will perhaps also serve to illustrate more generally the paths followed by other collections of this type in the United Kingdom and Eire over the past hundred years. It has been encouraging to discover that far less has gone abroad than was previously supposed and that far more has merely moved unremarked into libraries and record offices throughout this country where it has assumed a fresh and perhaps less familiar identity.

The Commission's warmest gratitude is due to the many present owners and custodians of collections, both in this country and abroad, for the unfailing generosity and patience with which they have responded to requests for information on points of detail about their holdings.

Although virtually every member of the Commission's staff has contributed to the Guide's compilation, most of the research for it was carried out by Dr Isabel Kenrick. It has been edited for publication by Dr Eileen Scarff.

GRC DAVIS
Secretary
31 December 1981

Contents

Bibliographical note

The contents of the Reports and Calendars published by the Commission before 1957 are listed most comprehensively by ELC Mullins, *Texts and Calendars: an analytical guide to serial publications*, Royal Historical Society Guides and Handbooks, No 7, 1958, pp61-90. A short list is published annually by Her Majesty's Stationery Office *Sectional List 17: Publications of the Royal Commission on Historical Manuscripts*.

The bibliography of the Reports and Calendars series has long been confusing.

The Commission's earliest accounts of collections of historical papers were published as appendices to its periodical reports to the Crown. Nine such reports accompanied by appendices of this type appeared between 1870 and 1884 in seventeen folio parts. These dealt with a total of 424 collections.

Thereafter the format of the series was changed from folio to octavo and the 48 appendices to the 10th-15th Reports published between 1885 and 1899 were issued separately in parts as each was completed.

In 1883 publication was also started of octavo calendars of important individual collections of papers bearing the titles of the collections alone. The first such calendar dealt with the Salisbury (Cecil) MSS at Hatfield House and was completed in twenty four volumes in 1976.

Since 1899 all reports on collections have been presented in this revised form and the practice of dealing with them in appendices has entirely ceased.

Serial numbers were introduced in 1914 to bring together volumes dealing with the same collection but published under different titles at wide intervals. By this means the four volumes of the calendar of the MSS of the Duke of Portland published between 1891 and 1897 as appendices to the 13th, 14th and 15th Reports could be brought together with the six further volumes published between 1899 and 1931 as *Portland* V-X under the single serial number [29]. Since the serial numbers were applied retrospectively they do not appear on any volumes published before 1914 and were often omitted from later ones. They cannot therefore be regarded as forming part of any conventional bibliographical reference. In the present Guide they have been inserted after these references in square brackets.

Each volume or group of volumes in the Reports and Calendars series is separately indexed. But these indexes are also amalgamated in the *Guide to the reports of the Royal Commission on Historical Manuscripts*, Part I *Topographical: Reports issued 1870-1911* (1914); *1911-1957* (1973). Part II *Index of Persons: Reports issued 1870-1911*, 2 vols (1935, 1938); *1911-1957*, 3 vols (1966).

Access to privately owned collections of papers

Privately owned collections of papers that have been deposited on loan by their owners in libraries, record offices and other public institutions are normally available for research without restriction. Special conditions, however, may sometimes apply to their use, particularly if they are to be cited in published works. All enquiries on this point should be addressed to the institutions concerned.

Permission to see other privately owned collections should, in the first instance, be sought from their owners in writing. Applicants are reminded that such papers can normally be made available for use only at considerable personal inconvenience and expense to their owners, and that access for purposes of research is a privilege not a right. The conditions of access to individual collections were those prevailing in December 1980. Enquiries about papers described simply as 'in family possession' should be addressed to the Commission itself. For collections remaining in private possession in Scotland, enquiries may also be addressed to the National Register of Archives (Scotland).

Abbreviations

Gifts and Deposits	*Scottish Record Office, List of Gifts and Deposits* i-ii, Edinburgh 1971, 1976.
Ker, *Medieval Libraries*	NR Ker, *Medieval libraries of Great Britain: a list of surviving books*, Royal Historical Society Guides and Handbooks, No 3, 2nd edn 1964.
Ker, *Medieval MSS*	NR Ker, *Medieval MSS in British libraries*, i *London*, ii *Abbotsford-Keele*, Oxford, 1969, 1977.
[NRA]	Unpublished lists of papers of which copies are available for consultation in the National Register of Archives. The lists are cited in the Guide by their file number there, eg [NRA 6749]. Other copies however may be expected to be available in the hands of the owners of the documents concerned or of the libraries and record offices where they are lodged.

The location of collections described in the Reports & Calendars series

ABERDARE MSS see Davies, DP Esq

ABERDEEN, Burgh of
1870
First R, xii and App 121-23 [1]

In Aberdeen District Archives except the register of sasines from 1679, transferred to the Scottish Record Office.

ABERDEEN, University of
1871
Second R, xix-xx and App 199-201 [1]

Mostly in Aberdeen University Library. A few legal papers are held by the University Secretary. MR James, *Catalogue of the medieval MSS in the University Library, Aberdeen*, Cambridge, 1932. Ker, *Medieval MSS* ii, pp2-21.

ABERDEEN, Earl of
Haddo House, Aberdeenshire. 1876
Fifth R, xix and App 608-10 [4]

Presented to the Scottish Record Office in 1926 (GD 33) except the household book of James V 1538-39 (p608) and the account book of the 1st Earl 1682-84 (pp609-10). *Gifts and Deposits* i, pp74-76. Typescript inventory.
Some other family and estate papers remain at Haddo House [NRA 9758]. The papers of the 4th Earl of Aberdeen were presented to the British Museum in 1932 (Add MSS 43039-358, 51043), and those of the 1st Baron Stanmore in 1953 (Add MSS 49199-285. NRA 20961). The papers of the 1st Marquess were given to the Public Archives of Canada in 1952 [NRA 10477].

ABERGAVENNY, Marquess of
Eridge Castle, Sussex. 1885, 1887
Tenth R, 23-25 and App VI 1-72 [15]

Remain at Eridge Park, except five MS books and some documents (pp1-3) deposited in East Sussex RO with other estate and genealogical papers. Copies of the political papers of John Robinson (pp13-16) are held by the British Library (MS Facs 340(1)-(5)) which also has four volumes of his original parliamentary and private papers (Add MSS 37833-36). See further *Parliamentary papers of John Robinson 1774-84*, ed WT Laprade, Royal Historical Society, Camden Third Series xxxiii, 1922.
Some manorial and estate papers not noticed by the Report have been bought by the British Library (Add MS 60746) and others deposited with Sussex Archaeological Society [NRA 11856], in Gwent RO [partial list NRA 7410] and in Kent AO [NRA 7745]. Some stray family and estate papers are among the Spencer family papers at Althorp, not open for research [NRA 10410, pp51-63].

ABINGDON, Corporation of
1870, 1871
First R, App 98; Second R, xv and App 149-50 [1]

Remain with Abingdon Town Council except the mayor's book (p98) and chamberlains' accounts (pp149-50) which have been placed with other corporation records in Berkshire RO by gift or deposit at various dates since 1950 [NRA 4618].

ABINGDON, Hospital of Christ
1870
First R, App 98-99 [1]

Remain at Christ's Hospital, Long Alley Almshouses, St Helen's, Abingdon, Oxon.

ACLAND HOOD see Hood

AILESBURY, Marquess of
Savernake Forest, Wilts. 1898, 1899
Fifteenth R, 18-21 and App VII 152-306 [43]

Deposited with other family papers in
Wiltshire RO in 1975 except the diaries of
the 4th Earl of Ailesbury (pp269-306).
Some manorial documents were given to
Somerset RO and Wiltshire RO in 1946
[NRA 1399, 1550]. Household accounts of the
1st Earl of Ailesbury 1676-82 were deposited
in Bedfordshire RO in 1961. A cartulary of
Muchelney Abbey, Somerset was sold at
Christie's 16 Dec 1970 lot 17 and is now
British Library Add MS 56488.

AILSA, Marquess of
Culzean Castle, Ayrshire. 1876
Fifth R, xix and App 613-17 [4]

Presented to the Scottish Record Office 1943,
1946 (GD 25). Typescript inventory.

AINSLIE, Miss
Berwick upon Tweed, Northumberland. 1871
Second R, xii and App 68-69 [1]

The volume noticed, a compilation of London
customs, was sold to the British Museum in
1910 (Egerton MS 2885).

AIRLIE, Earl of
Cortachy Castle, Angus. 1871
Second R, xvii and App 186-88 [1]

Deposited in the Scottish Record Office,
1945 (GD 16). *Gifts and Deposits* i, pp20-26.
Typescript inventory.

AITKEN, George A Esq
Hornton Street, London W8. 1891
Twelfth R, App IX 334-42 [27]

The three letter books of Sir James Porter
have not been traced. Other copies of his
diplomatic letter books 1748-57 are among the
Hardwicke papers in the British Library
(Add MSS 35496-99).

ALDEBURGH, Corporation of
1907
Seventeenth R, 124-25; Various collections
IV 279-312 [55]

In Suffolk RO, Ipswich with other borough
records [NRA 10073].

ALEXANDER, W Cleverly Esq
Heathfield Park, Sussex. 1904
Sixteenth R, 117; Various collections
III 259-64 [55]

The letters of John Noyes MP and his wife
Alice were presented to the British Museum
in 1949 (Add MS 46842).

ALMACK, Richard Esq
Melford, Suffolk. 1870
First R, x and App 55 [1]

The Ely Priory register was acquired by the
Bishop of Ely in 1889 and deposited with the
Ely capitular records in Cambridge University
Library in 1970. William Penn's charter was
sold in 1893 and is now in the Pennsylvania
State Archives. The remainder were sold at
Sotheby's 11 Dec 1902 lots 442-642. A few
papers were resold at Sotheby's 20 May 1952
lots 271-73, including the copy of a letter to
Mary Queen of Scots and the letter from the
Duke of Lauderdale about the episcopacy
(lot 271), both bought by the National Library
of Scotland (MS 3922).

ALNWICK see Northumberland

ALWINGTON, Parish of
1876
Fifth R, xvi and App 597 [4]

Deposited in Devon RO in 1955 and 1979
[NRA Devon parish reports] apart from the
church rate book.

AMERICAN MSS see Royal Institution

AMPLEFORTH, St Lawrence's College
1871
Second R, xiii and App 109-10 [1]

Remain in the library at Ampleforth Abbey,
N Yorks. Ker, *Medieval MSS* ii, pp23-43.

ANCASTER, Earl of
Grimsthorpe, Lincs. 1892-1907
Thirteenth R, 31 and App VI 203-61 [32];
Seventeenth R, 55-68; Ancaster [66]

The papers noticed are mostly among the
family and estate papers deposited in
Lincolnshire AO at various dates since 1951.
Lincolnshire Archives Committee, *Archivists'
reports*, 1952-71 passim. Partial list
[NRA 5789]. The travel diary (pp418-24) and
a few other items have not been traced.
Some stray Bertie family papers were
auctioned at Sotheby's 22 June 1970 lots
313-71. Twelve lots were bought by
Lincolnshire AO which also holds twelve
further lots purchased by Lord Ancaster.
Some family and estate papers from
Drummond Castle 12th-19th cent were
deposited in the Scottish Record Office in 1954
(GD 160). Further estate papers 17th-19th cent
remain at Drummond Castle [NRA 20245].

ANTROBUS, JC Esq
Eaton Hall, Congleton, Cheshire. 1871
Second R, xi and App 69 [1]

Placed in the William Salt Library, Stafford
in 1938 where other family papers were
deposited in 1933 [NRA 0386].

ARBUTHNOTT, Viscount of
Arbuthnott House, Fordoun, Kincardineshire.
1881
Eighth R, xvii and App I 297-304 [7]

The missal, prayer book and psalter were sold
at Sotheby's 10 Dec 1897 and are now in
Paisley Museum. The remainder, apart from
one untraced MS treatise, were deposited in
Aberdeen University Library in 1969
[NRA 10014].

ARGYLL, Duke of
Inveraray Castle, Argyllshire. 1874, 1877
Fourth R, xix-xx and App 470-92 [3];
Sixth R, xvi-xvii and App 606-34 [5]

Remain at Inveraray Castle [NRA 9955]. Not
open for research.

ARUNDELL OF WARDOUR, Lord
Wardour Castle, Tisbury, Wilts. 1871
Second R, xii and App 33-36 [1]

Mostly in the possession of RJR Arundell Esq
at Wardour. The Latin Bible (p34) was sold
with a volume of sermons of H. de Erp at
Sotheby's 24 Nov 1947 lots 63-64, and is now
in the Pierpont Morgan Library, New York
(M 823).
    Some other Cornwall deeds 1580-1926 were
deposited by solicitors in Cornwall RO in
1965.

ASHBURNHAM, Earl of
Ashburnham Place, Sussex. 1881
Eighth R, App III [7]

The Stowe MSS (pp5-40) were sold to the
British Government in 1883 and are now in
the British Library except those in the Irish
language which are in the Royal Irish
Academy, Dublin.
    The MSS of Italian provenance in the
Libri collection (pp41-72), with ten Dante
MSS from the Appendix, were sold to the
Biblioteca Medicea-Laurenziana, Florence in
1884.
    166 MSS of French provenance in the
Libri and Barrois (pp72-99) collections were
sold to the Bibliothèque Nationale, Paris in
1887.
    The remainder of the Libri and Barrois
collections (some 538 MSS) were sold at
Sotheby's 10 June 1901. For the purchasers
see *Bibliothèque de l'Ecole des Chartes*, lxii,
1901, pp555-610; lxiii, 1902.

The additional MSS or 'Appendix'
(pp99-110) were sold privately to
Henry Yates Thompson in 1897, except the
Lindau Gospels (No 9) sold separately to the
Pierpont Morgan Library, New York in 1901.
For their subsequent dispersal see S De Ricci,
English collectors of books and MSS, 1930,
pp169-71, *British Museum Quarterly*, xvi,
1951-52, p46, *Times Literary Supplement*
20 May 1949.

ATHOLL, Duke of
Blair Atholl, Perthshire. 1879-90
Seventh R, xv-xvi and App 703-16 [6];
Twelfth R, 48-51 and App VIII 1-75 [26]

Remain at Blair Atholl with other family
papers [NRA 11000, 19071].

AXBRIDGE, Corporation of
1872
Third R, xx and App 300-08 [2]

At Axbridge Town Hall, Somerset in the
custody of the clerk to Axbridge Town Trust
[NRA 10400].

BACON FRANK see Frank

BAGOT, Lord
Blithfield, Staffs. 1874
Fourth R, xiv and App 325-44 [3]

Parts of the collection were sold at Sotheby's
26 Nov 1945 lot 128, 25 Feb 1946 lots 240-67
and 4 July 1955 lots 774-93. Eventual
recipients include the Folger Library,
Washington (the five vols of original letters,
pp329-38 and many of the unbound letters
pp341-42. NRA 20980), the National Library
of Scotland (the packet of letters about
Mary Queen of Scots, p341), the National
Maritime Museum (the volume of transcripts
of Lord Dartmouth's correspondence with the
Prince of Orange and copies of letters from
James II, p339), the Archives Nationales,
Paris (the copy of Walsingham's Negotiations,
p339) and Staffordshire RO.
    The Stafford MSS (pp325-28) and the
papers relating to Shropshire including the
letters on the Rye House plot (pp339,
341-44 passim) are among those deposited in,
and subsequently bought by Staffordshire RO
[NRA 5471].
    The order of Charles I 1645 (p341), further
17th cent copies of William Salisbury's
correspondence (cf p343) and some Welsh
estate papers were deposited in the National
Library of Wales in 1974.

BAGOT, Captain Josceline F
Levens Hall, Westmorland. 1885
Tenth R, 16-17 and App IV 318-47 [13]

Mostly remain at Levens Hall with other
family papers [NRA 6234]. Access through
Cumbria RO, Kendal. The book of hours
(pp346-47) and some 18th-19th cent
autograph letters were sold at Sotheby's
13 Dec 1900 and 21 June 1922 lots 644-91.
    Sir Charles Bagot's Canadian papers and
transcripts of his American and Russian papers
1816-43 were given to the Public Archives
of Canada in 1910.

BAILLIE COCHRANE see Cochrane

BAKER, WR Esq
Bayfordbury, Herts. 1871
Second R, xi and App 69-72 [1]

The letters and papers relating to
Jacob Tonson were largely dispersed by
auction at Sotheby's 25 Jan 1904, 7 Dec 1907
lots 150-68, 17 Dec 1924 lots 782-89, 1 July
1925 lots 771-89, and at Christie's 5 Nov 1945
lots 192-93. Eventual recipients include the
British Library (Egerton MS 2869), the
Pierpont Morgan Library, New York, the
Folger Library, Washington and the Clark
Memorial Library, Los Angeles.

BALFOUR, BRT Esq
Townley Hall, Drogheda, co Louth. 1885-92
Tenth R, 22 and App VI 252-58 [15];
Thirteenth R, 56

James II's book of devotions and James III's
marriage certificate (pp252-55) were acquired
in 1910 and 1964 by Trinity College, Dublin
(MSS 3529, 7574) which also bought other
Balfour deeds and papers with Townley Hall
in 1957 (MS 3771). The rest of the material
listed was deposited in the National Library of
Ireland with further family papers in 1958
[NRA 7570].
    The volume of Sir James Ware's MS
collections (Thirteenth R, p56) is in the
Victoria and Albert Museum Library
(Clements collection, Drawer 5).

BANKES, Ralph Esq
Kingston Lacy, Dorset. 1881
Eighth R, xiii and App I 208-13 [7]

Remain at Kingston Lacy. Not open for
research.
    Some other papers of Sir John Bankes
1630-40 were sold to the Bodleian Library,
Oxford in 1960 (R.6.64).

BANKS, William L Esq
Conway, Caerns. d.1893
Fifteenth R, 49; Sixteenth R, 134;
Welsh MSS II i 301-45 [48], 1899-1904

The Havod MSS noticed by the Reports
remain in Cardiff Central Library.

BANNATYNE, Mrs
Haldon, Devon. 1922, 1926
Nineteenth R, 32-35; Palk [74]

The papers of Sir Robert Palk 1767-86 were
given to Exeter City Library in 1922 and are
now in Devon RO with other family and estate
papers [NRA 11977]. The India Office
Library and Records holds a microfilm.
    Four further volumes of Sir Robert Palk's
papers were acquired by the British Museum
in 1894 (Add MSS 34685-88).

BARCLAY ALLARDICE, Mrs
Loyal House, Alyth, Perthshire. 1876
Fifth R, xx and App 629-32 [4]

Presented to the Scottish Record Office,
1942 (GD 49). *Gifts and Deposits* ii, pp35-36.
Typescript inventory.

BARNSTAPLE, Corporation of
1883
Ninth R, x-xi and App I 203-16 [8]

In the North Devon Athenaeum, Barnstaple
with other borough records [NRA 14271].

BARRETT LENNARD, Sir Thomas Bt
Belhus, Essex. 1892, 1904
Thirteenth R, App IV 365-77 [31];
Sixteenth R, 116; Various collections III
155-255 [55]

Deposited with other family papers in
Essex RO in 1945 [NRA 8987]. Some further
family and estate papers were added in 1973
from which the Berkshire manorial documents
and estate papers were transferred to
Berkshire RO in 1977.

BATH, Marquess of
Longleat, Wilts. 1872-1980
Third R, xiii-xiv and App 180-202 [2];
Fourth R, xii-xiii and App 227-51 [3];
Sixteenth R, 56-59; Seventeenth R, 35-45;
Eighteenth R, 85-89; Nineteenth R, 7;
Twenty-Third R, 8; Bath I-V [58]

Remain at Longleat. Enquiries to the librarian.

BATHURST, Earl
Cirencester Park, Glos. 1923, 1926
Nineteenth R, 35-39; Bathurst [76]

Deposited in the British Museum in 1965
(MS Loan 57. NRA 20952) except the
Miranda papers which were sold to
Venezuela in 1926 and some Pope and Swift
letters sold to the Pierpont Morgan Library,
New York.
　Other family and estate papers have been
deposited in Gloucestershire RO [NRA 6415].
Some Cirencester manorial documents
17th-20th cent are in the custody of Sewell,
Rawlins & Logie, solicitors, Cirencester
[NRA 4886].

BAYLY, JW Esq
Finglas, co Dublin. 1870
First R, xii and App 128 [1]

Sir Edward Walker's Short Journal of several
actions performed in the Kingdom of Scotland
was given to Edinburgh University Library in
1957 (DK.5.21). The two letters of Charles II
have not been traced.

BEAMONT, William Esq
Orford Hall, Lancs. 1874
Fourth R, xv and App 368 [3]

The original documents, with Mr Beamont's
copies, are in Warrington Public Library
[NRA 14602].

BEAUFORT, Duke of
Badminton House, Glos. 1890, 1891
Twelfth R, 12-13 and App IX 1-115 [27]

Remain at Badminton with other family
papers.
　Most of the English estate papers earlier
than 1875 have been deposited in
Gloucestershire RO with a few other papers
[NRA 6282]. The Welsh estate papers have
been deposited in the National Library of
Wales at various dates since 1940
[NRA 12100, 12101].

BECCLES, Corporation of
1914, 1917
Eighteenth R, 211-15; Various collections
VII 70-79 [55]

Kept at Beccles with other borough records in
the custody of Waveney District Council
[NRA 2988], apart from some of the
documents formerly in the possession of the
town clerk (p78) deposited in Suffolk RO,
Ipswich in 1959 and 1960
[NRA 7822 (HD 330)].

BEDFORD, Duke of
Woburn Abbey, Beds. 1871
Second R, ix and App 1-4 [1]

Remain in family possession. Enquiries to the
archivist, Bedford Settled Estates,
29A Montague Street, London WC1.
　Some estate papers have been deposited in
Bedfordshire RO [NRA 17140] and Devon RO
[NRA 9813] at various dates since 1964.
*Russell estate collections for Bedfordshire and
Devon to 1910*, Bedford County Council, 1966.

BEDINGFELD, Sir Henry Bt
Oxburgh Hall, Norfolk. 1872
Third R, xvi and App 237-40 [2]

Remain at Oxburgh Hall with other family
papers [NRA 5522]. Not open for research.

BELVOIR see Rutland

BERINGTON, Charles Michael Esq
Little Malvern Court, Worcs. 1871
Second R, xii-xiii and App 72-73 [1]

Deposited in Hereford and Worcester RO,
Worcester in 1947 [NRA 1325], except the
Nieuport Carthusian papers (p73) restored to
the Order at Parkminster, Sussex in 1887.

BERKELEY see Fitzhardinge

**BERWICK UPON TWEED,
Corporation of**
1872-1904
Third R, xxi and App 308-10 [2]; Sixteenth R,
93-94; Various collections I 1-28 [55]

Kept at the Council Offices,
Berwick upon Tweed with other corporation
records 16th-20th cent, in the joint custody of
the Northumberland County Archivist and the
Chief Executive of Berwick [NRA 7873].

BETHUNE, Sir John Bt
Kilconquhar House, Fife. 1876
Fifth R, xxi and App 623-26 [4]

Deposited in the Scottish Record Office, 1962
(GD 246).

BEVERLEY, Corporation of
1900, 1904
Sixteenth R, 91-93; Beverley [54]

At Beverley Guildhall. Many other corporation
records were deposited in Humberside RO in
1957. Typescript lists [NRA 6616].

BISHOP'S CASTLE, Corporation of
1885
Tenth R, 18-19 and App IV 399-407 [13]

Deposited in Shropshire RO, 1979
[NRA 2990].

BLAIRS, Catholic College of
1871
Second R, xx and App 201-03 [1]

Most of the material noticed was transferred to
the Scottish Catholic Archives, Columba
House, Edinburgh in 1958-60 [NRA 7865].
The six items retained were deposited in
1974-75 with the college library and other
MSS not noticed by the Report in the
National Library of Scotland [NRA 20740].
See further D McRoberts, 'The Scottish
Catholic Archives, 1560-1978', *Innes Review*,
xxviii, 1977, pp59-128. Ker, *Medieval MSS* ii,
pp113-29.

BLICKLING see Lothian

BOUVERIE PUSEY, Sidney EE Esq
Pusey House, Faringdon, Berks. 1879
Seventh R, App 681 [6]

Deposited in Berkshire RO, 1951. *Guide to the
Berkshire Record Office*, 1952, pp71-72.

See also: Pleydell Bouverie; Radnor

**BOYCOTT, the Misses Mary M and
Margaret A**
Hereford. 1885
Tenth R, 4-5 and App IV 210-23 [13]

Given to Hereford City Library, 1943.

BRADFORD, Earl of
Belgrave Square, London SW. 1871
Second R, ix and App 30 [1]

The Torrington papers described by the
Report remain in family possession at Weston
Park. Access through Staffordshire RO.

Some other family and estate papers, not
noticed by the Report, have been deposited at
various dates since 1896 in the William Salt
Library, Stafford [NRA 7953], Shropshire RO
[NRA 11197], Lincolnshire AO [NRA 9551],
Bolton Metropolitan Borough Archives
[NRA 18677], Lancashire RO and
Staffordshire RO.

BRAYBROOKE, Lord
Audley End, Essex. 1881
Eighth R, xii-xiii and App I 277-96 [7]

The fifty-nine volumes of American and
East Indian papers of Charles, 1st Marquess
Cornwallis (pp287-96) were presented

to the Public Record Office in 1880
(PRO 30/11/1-59), and further volumes were
given in 1947 (PRO 30/11/60-283)
[NRA 8658].

The remaining family and estate papers were
distributed as loans or gifts in 1947 between
the Public Record Office (PRO 30/50.
NRA 23642), Trinity House, London,
Essex RO (*Guide to the Essex RO*, 1969,
pp119-22. NRA 6803), Berkshire RO
[NRA 0431], and Cambridge University
Library (Doc 3810-12, 3896-98;
Add 7090-110). The last include the grants of
arms, the Walden Abbey survey, the
Duke of York's household book, and the
accounts of the 2nd Earl of Suffolk's debts.

BRAYE, Lord
Stanford Hall, Leics. 1885, 1887
Tenth R, 21-22 and App VI 104-252 [15]

Most of the papers noticed were dispersed by
sale at Sotheby's 2 Feb 1943 lot 502,
17 Feb 1947 lots 650-729 (some resold
25 July 1969 lots 401-02), 23 June 1952
lots 120-31, 25 June 1956 lots 760-65 and at
Christie's 23 June 1954 lots 108-12, or
privately. The Peck MSS and some Cave MSS
remain at Stanford Hall.

Of the Cave MSS, the deeds and legal
documents (p105) and the papers relating to
parliamentary elections and to Bridges's
History of Northamptonshire (p108) are now
among those deposited in Leicestershire RO
at various dates since 1953 [NRA 9254]. The
John Dowland lute commonplace book (p108)
is in the Osborn Collection, Beinecke Library,
Yale University (MS fb 162). The survey of
His Majesty's coastal forts 1636 (p110) is
British Library Add MS 56467.

Originals or photocopies of most of the
Browne MSS (pp118-87) were acquired by the
House of Lords Record Office between 1952
and 1968 (*Guide to the records of Parliament*,
1971, pp270-72. NRA 7116). John Browne's
commonplace book (pp119-24), with other
Browne MSS, is in the Osborn Collection at
Yale University [NRA 18661]. The volume of
Westminster Assembly papers (p119) is with
the United Reformed Church History Society,
London. The volume of letters and state
papers 1642-47 (pp145-67) was broken up
before sale at Sotheby's 17 Feb 1947 and its
contents have now become widely dispersed.

Francis Peck's transcript of MS Mordaunt
(pp118-216) is a copy of an original letter book
now in the John Rylands Library,
Manchester University (Spencer MSS). See
*The letter-book of John, Viscount Mordaunt,
1658-1660*, ed M Coate, Royal Historical
Society, Camden Third Series lxix, 1945.

The Stuart papers (pp216-52, Sotheby's
17 Feb 1947 lots 670-715) have become
divided between the Royal Archives, Windsor,
Inverness Museum and Art Gallery,

Chiddingstone Castle, Kent, the Houghton Library, Harvard University, and various private collections.

BREADALBANE, Marquess of
1874
Fourth R, xxii and App 511-14 [3]

Mostly presented or sold to the Scottish Record Office at various dates since 1926 (GD 112). Typescript inventory. Three bundles of writs and autograph letters are in private possession [NRA 20973].

A few 18th cent family papers are held by Thompson, Dickson & Shaw WS, Edinburgh [NRA 10441]. A household book 1650-71 is in Glasgow University Library.

BRIDGNORTH, Corporation of
1885
Tenth R, 20 and App IV 424-37 [13]

Deposited in Shropshire RO, 1979.

BRIDGWATER, Corporation of
1870, 1872
First R, App 99 [1]; Third R, xix-xx and App 310-20 [2]

Deposited in Somerset RO in 1967 apart from the royal charters which remain in Bridgwater Town Hall in the custody of Sedgemoor District Council. TB Dilks, *Bridgwater borough archives 1200-1468*, Somerset Record Society, xlviii, liii, lviii, lx, 4 vols, 1933-48, and *Calendar of some medieval MSS . . .*, Somerset Record Society, lvii, 1942.

BRIDGWATER TRUST
Walkden, Lancs. 1887, 1888
Eleventh R, 24-26 and App VII 126-67 [22]

The papers noticed, mainly of Sir Thomas Egerton, Baron of Ellesmere and Viscount Brackley, were sold with much other material from Bridgwater House, London to Henry E Huntington in 1917 and are now in the Huntington Library, San Marino.

Further papers descended to the Duke of Sutherland and are at Mertoun. Copies of a calendar of both groups made c1900 are held by the Huntington Library, the National Library of Scotland and Cambridge University Library [NRA 24601].

Other records of the Brackley estate down to 1803 are deposited in Northamptonshire RO [NRA 4357].

BRIDPORT, Corporation of
1877
Sixth R, App 475-98 [5]

Deposited in Dorset RO, 1966 [NRA 3704]. T Wainwright, *Bridport records and ancient MSS*, 1900. ES Scroggs, *Brief guide to the municipal records of Bridport*, 1953. Ker, *Medieval MSS* ii, pp169-73.

BRISTOL, Dean and Chapter of
1870
First R, App 97-98 [1]

The single item noticed, a register of leases 1542-73, remains at the cathedral. Most of the other capitular records have been deposited in Bristol RO at various dates since 1959 [NRA 9846]. IM Kirby, *Catalogue of the records of the bishop and archdeacons and of the dean and chapter of the diocese of Bristol*, Bristol, 1970.

BRITISH MUSEUM (Welsh MSS)
1899, 1910
Fifteenth R, 47-49; Seventeenth R, 159; Welsh MSS II iv [48]

In the British Library.

BROGYNTYN see Ormsby Gore

BROMLEY DAVENPORT, W Esq
Baginton Hall, Warwicks and Capesthorne Hall, Cheshire. 1871, 1887
Second R, xi and App 78-81 [1]; Tenth R, 20 and App VI 98-103 [15]

Mostly dispersed by auction at Sotheby's 8 May 1903 (Baginton), 10 May 1907 (Capesthorne, Baginton), 7 and 27 Oct 1947 lots 259-60, 304-431, and by private sales. Some items were resold at Hodgson's 29 Jan 1909, 30 Mar 1916, and at Sotheby's 4 July 1955 (de Coppet). The residue was deposited in the John Rylands Library, Manchester University with other family and estate papers (*Annual reports* 1952, 1955, 1957. NRA 0592).

Eventual recipients of items sold include the British Library (Add MSS 36791-95, 36824-68), Keele University Library (in the Raymond Richards collection. Partial list NRA 1085), Harvard University Law School Library, Cambridge, Massachusetts, the Bodleian Library (MSS.Lat.misc.c.66; Eng.theol.f.27) and the Guildhall Library, London.

BROWNE, George Esq
Town End, Troutbeck, Westmorland. 1885
Tenth R, 17 and App IV 347-58 [13]

Deposited in Cumbria RO, Kendal in 1963 with other family papers except the book of devotions of Thomas Percy, 7th Earl of Northumberland (pp357-58), sold to the 7th Duke of Northumberland in 1905.

BRUCE, Sir Hervey JL Bt
Clifton Hall, Notts. 1914, 1917
Eighteenth R, 225-26; Various collections
VII 247-96, 389-433 [55]

Deposited in Nottingham University Library,
1948, 1958 [NRA 1022].

BRUMELL, Francis Esq
Morpeth, Northumberland. 1877
Sixth R, App 538-40 [5]

Deposited with the Society of Antiquaries of
Newcastle upon Tyne in 1901 and transferred
to Northumberland RO in 1961.

**BUCCLEUCH AND QUEENSBERRY,
Duke of**
Drumlanrig Castle, Dumfriesshire. 1872-1903
Third R, App 402 [2]; Fifteenth R, 43-44 and
App VIII; Sixteenth R, 117-22; Drumlanrig
II [44]

Remain at Drumlanrig Castle [NRA 6184].
  The Melrose Abbey charters 1124-1625
from Bowhill House were deposited in the
Scottish Record Office in 1952 (GD 55) and
the Buccleuch muniments 14th-20th cent from
Dalkeith Palace in 1967 (GD 224). The
Charles Townshend papers were subsequently
withdrawn from the latter deposit and sold to
the William L Clements Library, University
of Michigan in 1976 (British Library
microfilm M/730(1-3)). The papers relating to
Boughton House were transferred to
Northamptonshire RO. Further family and
estate papers remain at Bowhill [NRA 6184].

**BUCCLEUCH AND QUEENSBERRY,
Duke of**
Montagu House, London SW1. 1899-1928
Sixteenth R, 29-47; Twentieth R, 5;
Buccleuch (Montagu House) I-III [45]

Deposited on loan in Northamptonshire RO
since 1965 except the Winwood papers
(I, pp1-212), the Montagu-Arlington letters and
the Holles MSS (ibid, pp418-542) all kept
since 1917 at Boughton House. Access
through Northamptonshire RO.
  Other papers from Montagu House not
referred to in the Report include wardrobe
accounts c1660-1750 presented to the Royal
Archives, Windsor in 1917, and estate papers
for various counties deposited in
Northamptonshire RO [partial list
NRA 23059] which also has letters and papers
of the 2nd Duke of Albemarle 1673-88 on
temporary loan [NRA 20194].
See also: Montagu of Beaulieu

BUCHAN, James Esq
Auchmacoy House, Ellon, Aberdeenshire. 1874
Fourth R, xxiii and App 528-29 [3]

Remain at Auchmacoy House [NRA 9755].

BUCKIE see Kyle

BUCKINGHAMSHIRE, Earl of
Great Hampden, Bucks. 1895, 1896
Fourteenth R, 23-25 and App IX 1-154 [38]

Deposited with other family and estate papers
in Buckinghamshire RO, 1950 [NRA 0001].
  Some deeds of the family's London
properties were deposited in the Greater
London RO in 1953.
See also: Lothian (Blickling)

BUNBURY, Sir Charles Bt
Bury, Suffolk. 1872
Third R, xvi and App 240-42 [2]

Mostly dispersed by auction at Sotheby's
2 July 1896 various lots, 18 Apr 1932 lot 220,
27 Feb 1933 lots 206-16, or by private sale
in 1904. The residue including the Mildenhall
court rolls and Sir HE Bunbury's 19th cent
militia papers was deposited in Suffolk RO,
Bury St Edmunds in 1949 [NRA 2582].
  The Bury St Edmunds register and a
Mildenhall compotus are now in Cambridge
University Library (Add 4220-21). The
reports of Star Chamber cases (2 vols) and the
treatise on the officers of the Exchequer are in
the Folger Library, Washington.
  A small parcel of letters to Sir HE Bunbury
is in the British Library (Add MS 42863).

BURFORD, Corporation of
1901, 1904
Sixteenth R, 94-95; Various collections
I 29-64 [55]

Deposited by the trustees in the Tolsey
Museum, Burford, 1960 [NRA 5480].
RH Gretton, *Burford records*, Oxford, 1920.

BURNETT, Sir James Horn Bt
Crathes Castle, Kincardineshire. 1871
Second R, xix and App 197 [1]

Remain at Crathes Castle in the custody of the
National Trust for Scotland [NRA 10120]
except the court book of the Barony of Skene,
deposited in the Scottish Record Office in
1952 (GD 1/299).

BURNETT family
Fordoun House, Kincardineshire. 1874, 1877
Fourth R, xxii and App 518-21 (James
Burnett) [3]; Sixth R, xviii and App 673-81
(Arthur Burnett) [5]

The papers of James Burnett, Lord Monboddo
were sold to the National Library of Scotland
in 1973 (Acc 5738).

BURY ST EDMUNDS, Corporation of
1895, 1896
Fourteenth R, 41 and App VIII 121-58 [37]

Deposited in Suffolk RO, Bury St Edmunds
except the four medieval MSS noticed on
pp121-22. Of these, No I was sold privately
to the Wellcome Institute in 1971. Nos II-IV
were sold at Sotheby's 12 July 1971 lots
35A-37. No II was bought for the Huntington
Library, San Marino (HM 35300), No III
(Peter Lombard's Commentary, wrongly
ascribed by the Report to Bede) was bought
for the Bibliothèque Royale, Brussels and
No IV for Leiden University Library
(British Library microfilm RP 657).

BUTE, Marquess of
Eccleston Square, London SW and
Mountstuart, Isle of Bute. 1872, 1876
Third R, xiii, xxii and App 202-09, 402-03 [2];
Fifth R, xix and App 617-20 [4]

Mostly remain at Mountstuart with other
papers of the 3rd Earl of Bute bought back in
1939 [Partial list NRA 15459]. A few MSS
have been sold privately. George Owen's
Description of Pembrokeshire and the volume
of Cornish miracle plays, Welsh poetry etc
(pp202-03, 207) were bought by the National
Library of Wales in 1972 and 1973
(MSS 13212, 21001). The William Hack
volume (p208) was bought by AA Houghton
and resold at Christie's 13 June 1979, lot 244.
   Other family papers, including Glamorgan
and Monmouthshire manorial records and
Cardiff borough records, were deposited in the
National Library of Wales in 1950
[NRA 0581]. Some correspondence of the
3rd Earl is in Cardiff Central Library. Further
estate and business papers 18th-19th cent
were given to Glamorgan Archive Service
[NRA 10781]. The Luton Hoo estate papers
among these were transferred to
Bedfordshire RO in 1965 and 1967
[NRA 10481]. Some MSS were sold at
Sotheby's 30 Oct 1950 lots 122-23, 268-71.
   Another group of family papers which
descended to the Earl of Harrowby remains at
Sandon Hall [NRA 1561], apart from the

diplomatic correspondence of the 3rd Earl
and the 1st Marquess which was sold at
Sotheby's 13 June 1903 and is now British
Library Add MSS 36796-814.

BUXTON, Miss M
Shadwell Court, Norfolk. 1903, 1904
Sixteenth R, 105-07; Various collections
II 227-88 [55]

Mostly presented to Cambridge University
Library at various dates since 1901 with other
family and estate papers. The manorial extent
of Rushworth 1271 and the Eyke Chantry
foundation deed 1351 (p228) which were
retained by A Jessopp are now in Norfolk RO
[NRA 17984].

CALTHORPE, Lord
Grosvenor Square, London W1. 1871
Second R, x-xi and App 39-46 [1]

The Yelverton MSS described by the Report
were bought as a collection for the British
Museum in 1953 (Add MSS 48000-196).

CAMBRIDGE, Corporation of
1870
First R, App 99-100 [1]

Deposited with other corporation records in
Cambridgeshire RO at various dates since
1970.

CAMBRIDGE, University Registry
1870
First R, App 73-74 [1]

In the custody of the Keeper of the
University Archives at Cambridge University
Library [NRA 7134]. HE Peek and CP Hall,
*Archives of the University of Cambridge; an
historical introduction*, Cambridge, 1962.
Typescript lists and indexes.

CAMBRIDGE, Christ's College*
1870
First R, App 63 [1]

At the college in the custody of the archivist.

CAMBRIDGE, Clare College*
1871
Second R, xiii-xiv and App 110-16 [1]

At the college in the custody of the bursar.

---

*Most of the reports on the holdings of Cambridge colleges deal only with their archives. Their MS
collections have been described more recently by ANL Munby, Cambridge college libraries, 2nd edn,
Cambridge, 1962.*

CAMBRIDGE, Corpus Christi College*
1870
First R, App 64-67 [1]
At the college in the custody of the
librarian. For the MSS see also R Vaughan
and J Fines 'Handlist of MSS in the library of
Corpus Christi College, Cambridge, not
described by MR James', *Cambridge
Bibliographical Society Transactions*, iii, pt 2,
1960, pp113-23.

CAMBRIDGE, Downing College*
1872
Third R, xx-xxi and App 320-27 [2]
The John Bowtell antiquarian collection
described by the Report remains in the
college library [NRA 22707].

CAMBRIDGE, Emmanuel College*
1874
Fourth R, xviii and App 417-21 [3]
At the college in the custody of the archivist.
Typescript handlist.

**CAMBRIDGE, Gonville and
Caius College***
1871
Second R, xiv and App 116-18 [1]
At the college in the custody of the bursar.

CAMBRIDGE, Jesus College*
1871
Second R, xiv and App 118-21 [1]
At the college in the care of the keeper of
the records.

CAMBRIDGE, King's College*
1870
First R, App 67-69 [1]
At the college in the custody of the archivist.
J Saltmarsh, 'Muniments of King's College',
Cambridge Antiquarian Society Proceedings,
xxxiii, 1933, and 'Handlist of the estates of
King's College, Cambridge', *Bulletin of the
Institute of Historical Research*, xii, 1934,
pp32-38. Handlist of the deeds of the Priory
of St James by Exeter [NRA 3643].

CAMBRIDGE, Magdalene College*
1876-1917
Fifth R, xv-xvi and App 481-84 [4];
Eighteenth R, 21-34; Pepys [70]
Remain at the college, the archives in the
custody of the bursar and the Pepys MSS
with the Pepys Librarian.

JR Tanner and others, *Descriptive catalogue of
the naval MSS in the Pepysian Library at
Magdalene College, Cambridge*, Navy Records
Society, xxvi, xxvii, xxxvi, lvii, 4 vols, 1903-23.

CAMBRIDGE, Pembroke College*
1870, 1876
First R, App 69-72 [1]; Fifth R, xvi and
App 484-88 [4]
At the college in the custody of the librarian.
Typescript catalogue.

CAMBRIDGE, Peterhouse*
1870
First R, App 77-82 [1]
At the college in the custody of the archivist.

CAMBRIDGE, Queens' College*
1870
First R, App 72-73 [1]
Deposited in the university library, 1968.
JF Williams, 'The muniments of Queens'
College', *Cambridge Antiquarian Society
Proceedings*, xxvii, 1926, pp43-48. Typescript
handlist.

CAMBRIDGE, St Catharine's College*
1874
Fourth R, xvii-xviii and App 421-28 [3]
At the college in the custody of the archivist.
Typescript catalogue.

CAMBRIDGE, St John's College*
1870
First R, App 74-77 [1]
At the college in the custody of the archivist.

CAMBRIDGE, Sidney Sussex College*
1872
Third R, xx and App 327-29 [2]
At the college in the custody of the archivist.

CAMBRIDGE, Trinity College*
1870
First R, App 82-86 [1]
At the college in the custody of the librarian.

CAMBRIDGE, Trinity Hall*
1872
Second R, xiv and App 121-23 [1]
At the college in the custody of the librarian.
Typescript list of the muniments down to
1600.

---

*Most of the reports on the holdings of Cambridge colleges deal only with their archives. Their MS
collections have been described more recently by ANL Munby, Cambridge college libraries, 2nd edn,
Cambridge, 1962.*

CAMOYS, Lord
Stonor Park, Henley on Thames, Oxon. 1871
Second R, xii and App 33 [1]

The single MS noticed was sold at Sotheby's
29 June 1938 lot 523 and is now in the
University of Pennsylvania Library
(MS Eng 8).

Another MS was included in the sale of
books from the library at Stonor Park,
Sotheby's 3 Aug 1939 lot 257. The family
papers otherwise remain at Stonor Park
[NRA 1026].

CANTERBURY, Dean and Chapter of
1877-1904
Fifth R, xii-xiv and App 426-62 [4];
Eighth R, xiv-xv and App I 315-55 [7];
Ninth R, viii and App I 72-129 [8];
Sixteenth R, 99-100; Various collections
I 205-81 [55]

In Canterbury Cathedral Library and City RO.
CE Woodruff, *Catalogue of the MS books in the
library of Christchurch, Canterbury*, 1911.
Ker, *Medieval MSS* ii, pp265-330.

**CANTERBURY, Black Book of the
Archdeacon**
1877
Sixth R, App 498-99 [5]

In Canterbury Cathedral Library and City RO.
CE Woodruff, *Records of the courts of the
archdeaconry and consistory of Canterbury*,
Kent Archaeological Society, xli, 1929,
pp89-105.

CANTERBURY, Corporation of
1883
Ninth R, ix-x and App I 129-77 [8]

In Canterbury Cathedral Library and City RO.

CARDIFF FREE LIBRARY
1902-04
Fifteenth R, 47-49; Sixteenth R, 134;
Welsh MSS II i 91-300, ii 783-93 [48]

Remain in Cardiff Central Library. A further
fifty-eight Phillipps MSS bought by it in
1896 are noticed in the National Library of
Wales *Calendar of Wynn (of Gwydir) papers
1515-1690*, 1926.

See also: Banks

CAREW, Lt-Colonel GHW
Crowcombe Court, Somerset. 1871, 1874
Second R, xiii and App 74-76 [1]; Fourth R,
xv and App 368-74 [3]

The Grimbald Gospels were bought by the
British Museum in 1896 (Add MS 34890).
Most of the other MSS noticed were sold

at Sotheby's 6 May 1903 (156 lots).
Eventual recipients include the British
Library (Add MSS 36773-89, 40085-91), the
National Library of Wales (50 items mostly of
parliamentary interest among the Llangibby
Castle MSS), Trinity College, Dublin
(Sir James Ware's antiquarian collections) and
Sir John Gawen Carew Pole (the book
relating to the Order of the Garter.
NRA 5960).

Walsingham's journal (Fourth R, p369)
remains in the Public Record Office with
other volumes of Irish interest (PRO 30/5).

Other groups of family papers have been
deposited in Somerset RO and in Dyfed
Archives, Haverfordwest [NRA 23930] at
various dates since 1961.

CARISBROOKE, Parish of
1877
Sixth R, xiv and App 499-500 [5]

Deposited in the Isle of Wight County RO,
1971 [NRA Isle of Wight parish reports].

CARLISLE, Diocesan Registry
1883
Ninth R, ix and App 177-97 [8]

Deposited with other diocesan records in
Cumbria RO, Carlisle at various dates
since 1957.

CARLISLE, Dean and Chapter of
1871
Second R, xiii and App 123-25 [1]

The fourteen volumes noticed by the Report
remain with other capitular records in the
dean and chapter library. Access through
Cumbria RO, Carlisle.

CARLISLE, Corporation of
1883
Ninth R, ix and App I 197-203 [8]

Deposited in Cumbria RO, Carlisle
[NRA 24587].

CARLISLE, Earl of
Castle Howard, Yorks. 1897, 1899
Fifteenth R, 27-30 and App VI [42]

Mostly remain at Castle Howard in the
possession of George Howard Esq
[NRA 24681]. Nine of the MSS noticed
(pp xxvii-xxviii, 1-2) were included among
others from Castle Howard sold at Hodgson's
20 July 1944 lots 230-48. The Gilling MS
and the Liber Florum are now Bodleian
Library MSS. Lyell Empt. 22 and
Lat.misc.d.30. The metrical Life of
St Cuthbert is British Library Egerton
MS 3309. The sermons of Richard the Hermit

are in the Pierpont Morgan Library,
New York (M 872). Gower's Confessio
Amantis is Newberry Library, Chicago
MS Silver 3.

Some other MSS were included in sales of
books from Naworth Castle at Sotheby's
11 Apr 1927 lots 744-70 passim, 27 Oct 1947
lots 261-533 passim.

Groups of family deeds and manorial
documents for Cumberland were deposited
in Durham University, Department of
Palaeography and Diplomatic in 1954 and
1960 [NRA 11493].

CARR ELLISON, JR Esq
Dunston Hill, co Durham. 1899
Fifteenth R, 40-41 and App X 92-100 [47]

Mostly deposited in Northumberland RO,
1965 [NRA 7841].

CARRUTHERS see Erskine Murray,
Alexander Esq

CASTLE HOWARD see Carlisle, Earl of

CATHCART, Earl
Thornton le Street, Yorks. 1871
Second R, x and App 24-30 [1]

Remain in family possession at Auchindoune,
Nairn with other family papers [NRA 3946].

Some Yorkshire estate and business papers
were deposited in Leeds Archives Department
and in North Yorkshire RO in 1970.

CAULFIELD, Dr Richard
Cork. 1870
First R, xii and App 129 [1]

Sold following Caulfield's death in 1887.
The Cork deeds were given to Marsh's
Library, Dublin in 1941 (MS Z.1.1.18(21)).
The inventory of properties of the Galwey
family 1564 was given to the National
Library of Ireland in 1954 (MS 9034).

Other MSS from his antiquarian collection
including deeds and correspondence of the
Sarsfield family, Viscounts Kilmallock and
some Cork diocesan papers were bought by
Trinity College, Dublin in 1919
(MSS 2010-15. NRA 20233).

His own papers are in University College,
Cork (MS U 83). Two volumes of his
correspondence are in the Gilbert collection,
Dublin Public Libraries.

See also: Cork

CAWDOR, Earl
Cawdor Castle, Nairnshire. 1871
Second R, xvii and App 193 [1]

Remain at Cawdor Castle [NRA 8147].

CAWDOR, Earl
Stackpole Court, Pembs, until 1870
Second R, viii and App 31 [1]

The Golden Grove Book of Pedigrees
described by the Report was deposited in the
Public Record Office in 1870 and transferred
in 1978 to Dyfed Archives, Carmarthen, which
also holds other Vaughan family papers,
including another pedigree transferred there
in 1978 from the College of Arms
[NRA 21492].

CECIL see Salisbury, Marquess of

CHANDLER, R Powell Esq
College Court, Gloucester. 1890, 1891
Twelfth R, 47 and App IX 520-26 [27]

The records of the Butchers' gild, with which
the Report deals, are now in Gloucester
Central Library.

CHANDOS POLE GELL, Henry Esq
Hopton Hall, Derbys. 1884
Ninth R, xvii and App II 384-403 [8]

Most of the Gell family papers noticed by the
Report descended to Lt-Colonel John
Chandos Pole and were deposited by him in
Derbyshire RO in 1969 [partial list
NRA 10475], apart from some early deeds
and 18th cent papers which he retained at
Newnham Hall, Daventry, Northants. A few
items remain at Hopton Hall among the
papers of the cadet branch of the family
[NRA 5438].

CHARLEMONT, Earl of
1870-96
First R, xii and App 126-27 [1]; Twelfth R,
52 and App X; Thirteenth R, 56 and
App VIII [28]; Fourteenth R, 51-52

The seventeen volumes of memoirs and
correspondence of the 1st Earl are now in the
Royal Irish Academy, Dublin
(MSS 12.R.7, 9-24).

CHEDDAR, Parish of
1872
Third R, xix and App 329-31 [2]

The volume of accounts 1612-74 was presented
to Somerset Archaeological Society and is
now among its MS collections in
Somerset RO.

CHESTER, Corporation of
1881
Eighth R, xv-xvi and App I 355-403 [7]

In Chester City RO [NRA 23781].

CHICHESTER, Bishop of
1901, 1904
Sixteenth R, 96-97; Various collections
I 177-86 [55]

Deposited in West Sussex RO, 1951.
FW Steer and IM Kirby, *Catalogue of the records of the bishop, archdeacons and former exempt jurisdictions*, Chichester, 1966.

CHICHESTER, Dean and Chapter of
1901, 1904
Sixteenth R, 97-99; Various collections
I 187-204 [55]

Deposited in West Sussex RO at various dates since 1951. FW Steer and IM Kirby, *Catalogue of the records of the dean and chapter, vicars choral, St Mary's Hospital, colleges and schools*, Chichester, 1967.

CHICHESTER, Earl of
Stanmer Park, Sussex. 1872
Third R, xv and App 221-23 [2]

Among the papers presented to the British Museum, 1886-90 (Add MSS 32679-33201, 33320-44, 33617-31; Add Ch 29259-32739).

Groups of estate papers have also been acquired by Sussex Archaeological Society [NRA 10264], East Sussex RO [NRA 6751] and Hastings Museum and Art Gallery [NRA 1153]. The family papers which passed to the Clinton family, Dukes of Newcastle under Lyme are now in Nottingham University Library [NRA 7411].

CHISENHALE MARSH see Marsh

CHOLMONDELEY, Reginald Esq
Condover Hall, Salop. 1876
Fifth R, x and App 333-60 [4]

Sold with other papers at Puttick and Simpson's 24 Nov 1887 lots 975 and 976 and bought by Quaritch. Two thousand documents relating to the Smyth family of Nibley including most of those mentioned in the Report were sold on immediately to FA Crisp. The remainder were offered for sale in Quaritch's *Cat.* 87, Jan 1888. A few have subsequently reappeared in later sales eg Sotheby's 13 June 1945, 22 Oct 1956 (Crewe Hall sale) or have been resold privately.

Eventual recipients of sections of the Smyth of Nibley and Berkeley family papers have included Gloucester Central Library (FA Crisp's collections with additions. NRA 16645), Gloucestershire RO (the three volumes of Gloucestershire muster books bought by Lord Sherborne: p339), the British Library (Add MSS 33587-89, 34121), New York Public Library (the Virginia papers: pp340-41. NRA 20054), and the Folger Library, Washington (pp343-45 passim.

NRA 20054). Photocopies of some others owned privately by RM Willcocks are held by Gloucestershire RO [NRA 16645] and by the House of Lords Record Office [NRA 20336].

The Kingswood Abbey deeds (pp335-38) are now in Bristol University Library. The letters about Berkeley Castle (pp356-57) are at the Castle (access through the Gloucestershire County Archivist as Hon Archivist to the Berkeley Trustees).

The English poem on the Stations of the Cross (p334) is in the Newberry Library, Chicago and the Alchymical MS (p334) in Cambridge University Library (Add 4087). The two volumes of Collectanea Devana (p339b) are in Chester City Library. Most of the remainder of William Cowper's collections for Chester and the Isle of Man (pp338-40) are in Cheshire RO [NRA 6313].

CINQUE PORTS
1874
Fourth R, App 428 [3]

Deposited with other records of the Cinque Ports in Kent AO at various dates since 1960 [NRA 6744, 7737, 7740]. F Hull, *Calendar of the white and black books of the Cinque Ports, 1432-1955*, 1966. The royal charters of 1278 and 1364, and the Yarmouth books 1640-62 were transferred to Hastings Museum and Art Gallery in 1964.

CLARKE THORNHILL, TB Esq
Rushton Hall, Northants. 1904
Sixteenth R, 112-16; Various collections
III 1-154 [55]

Presented to the British Museum, 1919 (Add MSS 39828-38; Add Ch 62385-463).

Other family papers were deposited with the Yorkshire Archaeological Society, Leeds in 1932 and 1956 [NRA 3525].

CLAYTON, Sir William Bt
Harleyford House, Marlow, Bucks. 1907
Seventeenth R, 130; Various collections
IV 326-41 [55]

The sixty-seven medieval deeds noticed by the Report have been sold to or deposited in Surrey RO [NRA 8232], Devon RO [NRA 11454], Essex RO [NRA 5381], Leicestershire RO [NRA 23431] and the Guildhall Library, London (MS 2931).

Most of the family papers passed with Marden Park, Surrey to the Greenwell family c1900. They were later bought by GFT Sherwood and sold at Sotheby's 18 June 1928 lot 607, 25 Mar 1929 lots 395-412, and at Hodgson's 15 May 1929 lots 585-604. To the twenty-eight eventual recipients listed by FT Melton, *Bulletin of the Institute of Historical Research*, lii, 1979, pp91-98 are to be added the British Library (Add MS 45902(2)), Devon RO [NRA 11454], the Lewis Walpole Library, Farmington, Connecticut [NRA 22338] and the Shakespeare Birthplace Trust RO, Stratford upon Avon [NRA 4523]. His lists of items acquired by the Bodleian Library, Oxford, the Guildhall Library, London, Leicestershire RO and Lincolnshire AO are also incomplete.

The residues of the Clayton and Greenwell family papers have been placed in Buckinghamshire RO [NRA 5676] and in Surrey RO [NRA 8232, 8233].

CLEMENTS, MLS Esq
Ashfield Lodge, Cootehill, co Cavan. 1913, 1917
Eighteenth R, 95-101; Various collections VIII 196-568 [55]

The journal of the Irish House of Lords 1640-41 (pp200-14) was presented to the National Library of Ireland in 1959 (MS 2059) with other family papers.

The Molesworth correspondence (pp214-418) was sold at Sotheby's 12 Dec 1977 lot 106. A microfilm copy is held by the National Library of Ireland (n4681-82, p3752-53).

Other family papers were bought by Trinity College, Dublin in 1976 [NRA 18803]. For those still remaining in family possession see *National Library of Ireland report on private collections no 356*, typescript.

COCHRANE, ADR Baillie, 1st Baron Lamington
Lamington, Lanarkshire. 1876
Fifth R, xx and App 632-33 [4]

The four charters noticed relating to Wafralandis in Lanark have not been traced since Lamington House was sold in 1951.

Some other family papers have been presented to the National Library of Scotland (MSS 2264-505, 2568-608, 3022; Ch 945-46) and a few deposited by Tods, Murray & Jamieson WS of Edinburgh in the Scottish Record Office (GD 237).

COKE see Cowper, Earl

COLCHESTER, Lord
1872, 1874
Third R, xi [2]; Fourth R, xiv and App 344-47 [3]

Presented with other family papers to the Public Record Office, 1923, 1966 PRO 30/9. NRA 8652).

COLLIS, Mrs
1871
Second R, xiii and App 76-77 [1]

The papers of Thomas Sampson, dean of Christ Church, Oxford were sold to the British Museum in 1901 (Egerton MS 2836).

COPE, Revd Sir William, Bt
Bramshill House, Hants. 1872
Third R, xvi and App 242-44 [2]

Most of the MSS noticed were sold privately or by auction at Sotheby's 4 Mar 1913 (20 lots), 23 July 1923 lots 30, 38 and at Christie's 28 July 1971 lots 553-54, 5 Dec 1973 lot 90. A few which passed with Bramshill House to Lord Brocket in 1930 were sold at Sotheby's 14 July 1952 lots 137, 294-302.

The principal recipients include the British Library (Nos 10, 17, 18, 34, 35: Add MSS 38665-66, 40854-55; Egerton MS 3775), the Bodleian Library, Oxford (Nos 2, 21, 22, 31: MSS.Lat.th.d.46; Lyell Empt.11; Top.Oxon.c.454), Cambridge University Library (No 1: MS 5368), Keele University Library (Nos 23, 27: with the Raymond Richards collection), and a number of American libraries (Nos 4, 6, 12, 19, 20).

The family papers deposited in or bought by Hampshire RO include a few of the remaining volumes [NRA 0540].

CORBET, Sir Walter O Bt
Acton Reynald, Salop. 1899
Fifteenth R, 40 and App X 66-77 [47]

The deeds and other documents were deposited in Shropshire RO in 1950. *Guide to the Shropshire records*, 1952, pp74-76. Further estate papers were placed there in 1975 [NRA 21445].

CORBET, Revd JD
Sundorne, Salop. 1885
Tenth R, 19

The cartulary of Haughmond Abbey and the roll of statutes are now both in Shropshire Libraries Local Studies Department, Shrewsbury with other family and estate papers [NRA 9301]. Some further family papers are in Shropshire RO [NRA 11563].

CORBET, Richard Esq
Adderley, Salop. 1871
Second R, xi and App 77-78 [1]

The deeds noticed were deposited with other family and estate papers in Shropshire RO in 1950. *Guide to the Shropshire records*, 1952, pp77-80. Further estate papers were placed there in 1960 and 1975 [NRA 21445].

CORK, Corporation of
1870
First R, App 128-29 [1]

All the charters and registers noticed were destroyed or irreparably damaged in the Cork Courthouse fire of 1891, apart from a register of freemen 1656-1741 which was acquired by Cork City Library in 1973.

An original index to the council books 1710-1841 with a list of freemen has been deposited with the Cork Archives Council, Courthouse, Cork, which also holds the corporation minute books 1878-1929 [NRA 24548].

Extracts from the council books were printed by R Caulfield, *Council book of the corporation of Cork from 1609 to 1643, and from 1690 to 1800*, Guildford, 1876. Copies of the Court of D'Oyer Hundred book 1656-1729 and the apprentice enrolment book 1756-1801 are among Caulfield's own papers now in University College, Cork (MS U 83). His copy of the freemen's roll 1782-1850 is at Finbarre's Cathedral, Cork.

See also: Caulfield

COTTRELL DORMER, C Esq
Rousham, Oxon. 1871
Second R, xi and App 82-84 [1]

Remain at Rousham [NRA 0996].

COVENTRY, Corporation of
1870, 1899
First R, App 100-02 [1]; Fifteenth R, 43 and App X 101-60 [47]

In Coventry City RO. JC Jeaffreson, *Calendar of the books, charters . . . of the city of Coventry*, 1896. *Supplementary catalogue of the books and MSS added to the collection since the publication of JC Jeaffreson's catalogue of 1896*, 1931.

COVENTRY, Earl of
Croome Court, Worcs. 1870
First R, x and App 34 [1]

Lord Keeper Coventry's official papers were deposited in Birmingham Reference Library in 1938.

Most of the other family and estate papers remain at Croome Court [NRA 3843]. A few estate and lieutenancy papers have been deposited in Hereford and Worcester RO, Worcester at various dates since 1948 [NRA 0009, 1310]. The 13th cent cartulary of Stixwould Priory, Lincs that was sold at Sotheby's 25 Oct 1948 lot 127 is now British Library Add MS 46701.

COWPER, Earl
Melbourne Hall, Derbys. 1888-90
Twelfth R, 34-35 and App I-III [23]

Remain at Melbourne Hall in the possession of the Marquess of Lothian. Access through Derbyshire RO.

COWPER, Countess, and Baroness Lucas
Wrest Park, Shefford, Beds. 1871
Second R, ix and App 4-9 [1]

Most of the MSS were dispersed by auction at Sotheby's 19 June 1922 lots 565-643, 17 May 1926 lot 795 and Christie's 8 Nov 1978 lot 107, or by private sale, 1948-74.

Eventual recipients include the British Library (Add MSS 40671-74, 40676, 46918; Egerton MSS 3789-94), the Bodleian Library, Oxford (Nos 14, 17, 33, 42, 51), Spalding Gentlemen's Society (No 6), Glasgow University Library (No 8), the Guildhall Library, London (No 9), and various American libraries (Nos 3, 12, 13, 18, 25, 26, 44, 47).

The correspondence (p9) and Sir Anthony Benn's Essays (p8) are with the family papers deposited in Bedfordshire RO [NRA 6283]. Eight other MSS (Nos 4, 20, 21, 29, 41, 43, 48, 52) appear to remain in family possession.

The official papers of Thomas Robinson, Baron Grantham, were presented to the British Museum in 1860 (Add MSS 23780-830). Some further correspondence of the Robinson family was given by the 9th Baroness Lucas to Commander CG Vyner c1950 and is now in Leeds Archives Department [NRA 6160]. Another group of family deeds and papers is in York City Archives [NRA 11988].

See also: Ripon

CRAWFORD AND BALCARRES, Earl of
Dunecht, Aberdeenshire. 1871
Second R, xvii-xviii and App 181-82 [1]

Deposited in the John Rylands Library, Manchester University in 1956 where they rejoined the MSS from the Bibliotheca Lindesiana sold to Mrs Rylands in 1901 and the other groups of Lindsay family papers deposited there at various dates since 1946. *Handlist of personal papers from the muniments of the Earl of Crawford and Balcarres*, 1976.

CROMWELL RUSSELL see Prescott

CWRTMAWR see Davies, JH Esq

DALHOUSIE, Earl of
Brechin and Panmure Castles, Angus.
1870, 1871
First R, xii and App 117-19; Second R, ix,
xvii and App 186 [1]

Deposited with other family papers in the
Scottish Record Office at various dates since
1951 (GD 45). *Gifts and Deposits* ii, pp12-23
and typescript inventory. [Partial list
NRA 17164].

DALRYMPLE, Charles Esq
Newhailes, Midlothian. 1874
Fourth R, xxii and App 529-33 [3]

Included in the papers from Newhailes that
were accepted for the Nation in lieu of tax
and placed in the National Library of Scotland
in 1978 [NRA 17690].
    Other family papers were sold at Sotheby's
24 May 1937. Some estate papers were
deposited in the Scottish Record Office in
1962 [GD 246].

DALYELL, Sir Robert Alexander
Osborne Bt
The Binns, W Lothian. 1884
Ninth R, xix and App II 230-38 [8]

Remain at The Binns. Some other family
papers were presented to the Scottish Record
Office in 1964 (GD 241).

DANCEY, CH Esq
Midland Road, Gloucester. 1890, 1891
Twelfth R, 47 and App IX 526-29 [27]

The records of the Tanners' gild, with which
the Report deals, are in Gloucester Central
Library.

DARTMOUTH, Corporation of
1876
Fifth R, xvi and App 597-606 [4]

Deposited in Exeter City Library in 1939
and now in Devon RO.
    Some later records of the corporation have
been placed in West Devon Area RO,
Plymouth [NRA 22130].

DARTMOUTH, Earl of
Patshull House, Staffs. 1871-99
Second R, x and App 9-12 [1]; Eleventh R,
19-22 and App V (Dartmouth I) [20];
Thirteenth R, 32 and App IV 495-506 [31];
Fourteenth R, 25-27 and App X
(Dartmouth II); Fifteenth R, 30-35 and
App I (Dartmouth III) [20]

Many of the papers relating to Quebec,
Nova Scotia and Newfoundland
(Dartmouth I passim and Dartmouth II
pp545-606) were given to the Public Archives

of Canada in 1926 (MG 23 A1). Twenty-seven
volumes of naval papers (Dartmouth I
pp17-22, III pp5-106 passim) were deposited
in 1936 in the National Maritime Museum
which in 1951 also acquired a further volume
not noticed by the Reports (*Guide*, I, 1977,
pp106-07; *Journals and narratives of the
third Dutch War*, ed RC Anderson, Navy
Records Society, lxxxvi, 1946).
    A few items were included among the maps
and other papers sold at Sotheby's 9 Mar 1948
lots 433-71, 11 Nov 1963 lots 121-49,
2 Nov 1964 lots 350-58, or privately through
Quaritch (*Cat.* 660, 1948) and HP Kraus of
New York (*Cat.* 84, 23 Sept 1968). Eventual
recipients of these include the William L
Clements Library, University of Michigan
(Dartmouth II, p488, list of office holders in
America).
    Most of the remainder are among the
family papers deposited in Staffordshire RO
[NRA 5197, 8863], but many of the items
noticed in the Thirteenth Report have not
been traced.
    Further family and estate papers have been
deposited in Leeds Archives Department
[NRA 16328], Wakefield Archives Department
[NRA 23594], Hampshire RO [NRA 23200]
and the Greater London RO.

DARWIN, Francis Esq
Creskeld, Otley, Yorks. 1887, 1888
Eleventh R, 23 and App VII 90-93 [22]

Deposited with papers of the Darwin family
of Elston in Nottinghamshire RO, 1951
[NRA 5831].

DASENT, Sir George Webbe
1877
Sixth R, xiii and App 407-18 [5]

The single volume noticed, the cartulary of
the gild of St Peter upon Cornhill, London
1425-26, was sold at Sotheby's 30 Apr 1895
lot 443 and subsequently bought by the
Guildhall Library, London in 1947 (MS 4158).

DAVIES, DP Esq
Ynyslwyd, Aberdare, Glamorgan. 1902
Welsh MSS II i 395-408 [48]

Presented to the National Library of Wales,
1926 (MSS 5474-75A).

DAVIES JH Esq
Cwrtmawr, Llangeitho, Cardiganshire.
1899, 1905
Fifteenth R, 49; Welsh MSS II iii
871-937 [48]

Presented to the National Library of Wales,
1925-32.

DAVIES COOKE, Philip Bryan Esq
Owston, Yorks and Gwysaney, Flints. 1877
Sixth R, xv-xvi and App 418-26 [5]

Fifty-three of the fifty-seven MS books noticed by the Report were sold privately or by auction in 1959 (Sotheby's 1 June lots 390-402 and 15 June lots 197-215).

Eventual recipients include the National Library of Wales (the Liber Landavensis and twenty others of Welsh interest), Sheffield Central Library (No 15), the Bodleian Library, Oxford (Nos 5, 13, 16), and the Huntington Library, San Marino (Nos 2, 6, 19).

The family and estate papers from Gwysaney and Owston deposited in Clwyd RO, Hawarden at various dates since 1972 include fourteen of the documents noticed on pp421-26 [NRA 17586]. Others are among the papers from Gwysaney deposited in the National Library of Wales in 1942 or in the library of the University College of North Wales, Bangor in 1952 [NRA 8487]. Some further family and estate papers were deposited in Doncaster Archives Department in 1980. Others also remain in the Owston Park estate office [NRA 4430].

DELAVAL family, of Seaton Delaval
John Robinson Esq, Newcastle upon Tyne. 1892, 1893
Thirteenth R, 47 and App VI 186-202 [32]

Mostly returned to Seaton Delaval before 1918 and deposited by Lord Hastings in Northumberland RO in 1971. Further Delaval family papers that were given by John Robinson to the Society of Antiquaries of Newcastle upon Tyne and the North of England Institute of Mining and Mechanical Engineers have also been transferred to Northumberland RO at various dates since 1963 [Partial list NRA 10635].

See also: Waterford, Marchioness of

DE LA WARR, Earl
Buckhurst, East Grinstead, Sussex. 1872
Third R, xv and App 217-20 [2]

Mostly sold to the British Museum, 1906 (Add MSS 37341-97). A few letters and an account book 1537-40 (p217) have not been traced.

Other groups of family papers were deposited in East Sussex RO in 1960 and 1965 [NRA 14454].

See also: Sackville

DE L'ISLE AND DUDLEY, Lord and Viscount De L'Isle
Penshurst Place, Kent. 1872-1966
Third R, xvi and App 227-33 [2];
Twentieth R, 5-6; Twenty-First R, 13-14;
Twenty-Second R, 10; Twenty-Third R, 9;

Twenty-Fourth R, 7; De L'Isle and Dudley I-VI [77]

Deposited with other family papers in Kent AO, 1969 [NRA 17989]. A microfilm of the calendared MSS is held by the British Library (M/772).

DENBIGH, Earl of
Newnham Paddox, Rugby, Warwicks. 1874-1917
Fourth R, xvi and App 254-76 [3]; Sixth R, xi-xii and App 277-87 [5]; Seventh R, xiii and App 196-232 [6]; Eighth R, xi and App I 552-72 [7]; Eighteenth R, 58-69; Denbigh V [68]

The eleven letters from William Harvey to Lord Feilding (Denbigh V, pp28-41) were sold to Sir Thomas Barlow and presented to the Royal College of Physicians in 1912. The remainder were deposited in Warwickshire RO with other papers of the Feilding family and of the Pennant family of Downing Hall, Flints in 1980 [NRA 23684, 23685].

DE ROS, Lord
Old Court, Strangford, co Down. 1874
Fourth R, xiv and App 317-25 [3]

Deposited in the Public Record Office of Northern Ireland in 1952 [NRA 1178].

Some further letters to Lord Coningsby were sold with other family papers at Sotheby's 26 June 1972 lots 313-15 and 5 Feb 1973 lots 254-69. Eventual recipients include the Osborn Collection, Beinecke Library, Yale University, the Public Record Office of Northern Ireland and the British Library (Add MSS 57861-62).

DERRY, Diocesan Library
1881
Eighth R, App I 639-40 [7]

William Harrison's treatise on weights and measures and volumes 2, 3 and 4 of his 'Chronologie' have not been traced since used by FJ Furnivall for his edition of *Harrison's description of England in Shakspere's youth*, 3 vols, 1877-1908.

DESMOND see Fitzgibbon

DE TABLEY, Lord
Tabley House, Cheshire. 1870
First R, ix and App 46-50 [1]

Almost all the items noticed were given with other family papers to Cheshire RO in 1975 [NRA 3636].

Other MSS and muniments passed with Tabley House to the John Rylands Library, Manchester University in 1977. These included a copy (Eng MS 323) of the 17th cent volume of summons to Parliament noticed by the Report (p49a) which has not since been traced.

DEVON, Earl of
Powderham Castle, Devon. 1872, 1884
Third R, xv and App 216 [2]; Ninth R, App II 403-06 [8]

Mostly deposited in Devon RO in 1966 with other family and estate papers [NRA 13511]. Three literary and genealogical MSS (Third R) remain at Powderham Castle with a few historical documents.

DEVONSHIRE, Duke of
Hardwick Hall, Derbys and Bolton Abbey, Yorks. 1872
Third R, xiv-xv and App 36-45 [2]

Now all at Chatsworth House as the property of the Trustees of the Chatsworth Settlement [NRA 10821, 20594]. Access through the Librarian and Keeper of the Devonshire Collections, Chatsworth, Bakewell, Derbys.
    Some estate papers 17th-19th cent were deposited in Somerset RO in 1970 [NRA 17716].

DIGBY, George Wingfield Esq
Sherborne Castle, Dorset. 1881, 1885
Eighth R, xiii and App I 213-26 [7]; Tenth R, App I 520-617 [10]

The four volumes of correspondence noticed remain with other family papers at Sherborne Castle. The transcripts of the Earl of Bristol's papers 1605-95 (p213) are in the Public Record Office (PRO 31/8/198).
    The Dorset estate papers have been deposited in Dorset RO [NRA 1279] and the Warwickshire estate and family papers in Birmingham Reference Library [NRA 1280, 6208] at various dates since 1949.

DILKE, Sir Charles W Bt
Sloane Street, London. 1871
Second R, xvi and App 63 [1]

The MSS mentioned are now British Library Add MSS 28224-54, 28529, 28618-19; Add Ch 8793-9202, 18557-19062, 22614.

DILLON, Viscount
Dytchley, Charlbury, Oxon. 1871
Second R, x and App 31-33 [1]

The large folio Wycliffe's Gospels (p31) was presented to the British Museum in 1924 by the 17th Viscount (Add MS 41175). The history of the wars of Malta (p31) was included in the sale of printed books from the

Dytchley library, Sotheby's 12 June 1933 lot 65. The Spelsbury court rolls (p31) are among the Oxfordshire, Buckinghamshire and other estate and family papers deposited in Oxfordshire RO in 1935-36 [NRA 7176].
    The volume of thirty-nine letters from Charles II and James Duke of York to the Countess of Lichfield (p32) was sold at Sotheby's 17 June 1974 lot 160. A number of Jacobite letters including some of those noticed on pp32-33 have been sold singly at Sotheby's at various dates since 1976.
    The 16th Viscount's autograph collection, not noticed by the Report, was sold at Sotheby's 27 Feb 1893. The rest of the material remains in family possession.

DOD, Whitehall Esq
Llannerch, St Asaph, Flints. 1872
Third R, xviii-xix and App 258-60 [2]

Some of the material noticed is among the Gwysaney papers deposited in the National Library of Wales in 1947. The remainder has not been traced.

DONOUGHMORE, Earl of
Knocklofty, Clonmel, co Tipperary.
1890, 1891
Twelfth R, 35-38 and App IX 227-333 [27]

Deposited with other family papers in Trinity College, Dublin, 1980 [Partial list NRA 22331].

DOUGLAS, James Esq
Cavers House, Roxburghshire. 1879
Seventh R, xvi and App 726-32 [6]

Sold to the National Library of Scotland, 1976 [NRA 10136].

DOVASTON, John Esq
West Felton, Salop. 1892
Thirteenth R, App IV 247-82 [31]

The single volume noticed, containing a register of the Council of Wales and the Marches c1586-1634 and the Arguments de Shipmoney, was sold to the British Museum in 1909 (Egerton MSS 2882-83).
    Some other family and estate papers 18th-19th cent were deposited in Shropshire RO in 1966 [NRA 11563].

DOWNSHIRE, Marquess of
Easthampstead Park, Berks. 1924-
Nineteenth R, 16-22; Twenty-First R, 14; Twenty-Second R, 10; Downshire I-IV (V and VI in preparation) [75]

Sir William Trumbull's account of his Florentine embassy 1687 (Downshire I, pp240-48 passim) was sold with other unreported Trumbull MSS at Sotheby's 30 July 1963 lots 560-602 and bought, together with his diary, by the British Museum. (Add MSS 52279-80). Most of the other items from the sale are now in the Osborn Collection, Beinecke Library, Yale University (NRA 18661. British Library microfilms M/688, 690-91, 719; RP 22, 585, 708).

The rest of the material noticed by the Reports has been deposited in Berkshire RO with other family papers at various dates since 1954 [NRA 7133, 7580, 7864]. There is a microfilm copy of the Trumbull papers in the Library of Congress, Washington (*Checklist* D103-86).

The Irish estate papers were deposited in the Public Record Office of Northern Ireland in 1958 [NRA 21035].

DROGHEDA, Marquess of
Moore Abbey, Monasterevin, co Kildare. 1884
Ninth R, xix-xx and App II 293-330 [8]

Most were presented to the National Library of Ireland in 1943. A few remain untraced. See further *National Library of Ireland report on private collections no 100*, typescript [NRA 22978].

DROPMORE see Fortescue, JB Esq

DRYDEN, Sir Henry Bt
Canons Ashby, Northants. 1871
Second R, xi and App 63-64 [1]

The Elizabethan militia documents and Sir Henry Dryden's notes (p64b) were presented with his archaeological collections to Northampton Central Library in 1899. The folio missal (p64a) was sold to All Souls College, Oxford (MS 302) in the same year. The letters have been deposited with other family and estate papers in Northamptonshire RO [NRA 7634], apart from two sold at Sotheby's 17 Dec 1963 lot 466 and now in the Osborn Collection, Beinecke Library, Yale University (cf British Library MS Facs Suppl. x. 88).

DUBLIN, See of
1885
Tenth R, 43-44 and App V 204-19 [14]

The register Crede Mihi calendared by the Report remains with the Archbishop of Dublin. Access is through the diocesan archivist, Holy Cross College, Dublin.

DUBLIN, Corporation of
1870
First R, App 129 [1]

Remain at Dublin City Hall, in the care of the corporation archivist.

DUBLIN, Trinity College
1874, 1881
Fourth R, xxiv and App 588-99 [3];
Eighth R, xix and App I 572-624 [7]

Remain at the College. TK Abbott and EJ Gwynn, *Catalogue of the MSS in the library of Trinity College, Dublin*, Dublin, 1900, with a typescript continuation down to 1975 [NRA 19217] and a conspectus of catalogues [NRA 19810].

DUBLIN, College of the Irish Franciscans
1874-1907
Fourth R, xxiv and App 599-613 [3];
Seventeenth R, 153-59; Franciscan MSS [65]

In the Franciscan Library, Killiney, Dublin. M Dillon and others, *Catalogue of Irish MSS in the Franciscan Library, Killiney*, Dublin, 1969.

DUBLIN, Jesuit archives at see Ireland

DU CANE, Lady
Kilnwick Hall, Driffield, Yorks. 1905, 1907
Seventeenth R, 68-77; Du Cane [61]

Presented to Humberside RO in 1961 and 1976 with other papers of Vice-Admiral Henry Medley and the de Grimston family [NRA 13468].

DUNDAS, James Esq
Dundas Castle, W Lothian. 1872
Third R, xxiv and App 413-14 [2]

Sold to the Faculty of Advocates in 1924 and passed with its collections to the National Library of Scotland in 1925 (Adv MSS 80.1.1-80.7.14 (190 vols); Ch.B 41-1349).

Other family papers were presented to the Scottish Record Office in 1969 (GD 75). *Gifts and Deposits* ii, pp63-65. Typescript inventory.

DUNDAS, Robert Esq
Arniston, Gorebridge, Midlothian. 1872
Third R, xxiv-xxv and App 414-16 [2]

Remain at Arniston [NRA 8398]. A microfilm of some of the papers is held by the Scottish Record Office.

DUNNE, Major-General Francis Plunket
Brittas, Queens County. 1871
Second R, xx-xxi and App 227-31 [1]

The single volume noticed was sold at Sotheby's 19 Dec 1932 lot 182 and has not been traced.

DUNROBIN see Sutherland

DUNWICH, Corporation of
1914, 1917
Eighteenth R, 215-18; Various collections
VII 80-113 [55]

Deposited by Dunwich Town Trust in
Suffolk RO, Ipswich, 1967 [NRA 3979].

EDINBURGH, City of
1870
First R, App 126 [1]
In Edinburgh City Archives.

EDINBURGH, University of
1870-1928
First R, xii and App 121 [1]; Eighteenth R,
231-42; Twentieth R, 6; Laing I, II [72]

Remain in the University Library.
CR Borland, *Descriptive catalogue of the
western medieval MSS in Edinburgh
University Library*, Edinburgh, 1916. *Index to
the MSS in the University of Edinburgh
Library*, 2 vols, Boston, 1964.
Ker, *Medieval MSS* ii, pp589-624.

**EDINBURGH, Library of the Catholic
Bishop of**
1870
First R, xii and App 120-21 [1]

Transferred to the Scottish Catholic Archives,
Columba House, Edinburgh in 1958,
Fordun's Chronicon by direct deposit from
the Bishop's Library and the remainder with
the archives of Blairs College [Partial list,
1956 NRA 7865]. See further D McRoberts,
'The Scottish Catholic Archives, 1560-1978',
Innes Review, xxviii, 1977, pp59-128.

EDINBURGH, Advocates' Library
1870
First R, xii and App 123-26 [1]

Presented to the National Library of Scotland
on its foundation in 1925. *Summary catalogue
of the Advocates' MSS*, 1971.

EDMONSTONE family Bts
Duntreath, Stirlingshire. 1872-1917
Third R, xxiii and App 407-08
(Sir William Edmonstone) [2]; Eighteenth R,
247-51; Various collections V 72-184
(Sir Archibald Edmonstone) [55]

Deposited with other family papers in the
Scottish Record Office in 1957 (GD 57).
Typescript inventory. Section 3, the
correspondence calendared in Various
collections V, was subsequently withdrawn and

dispersed by auction at Sotheby's 26 Nov and
15 Dec 1980.

EFFINGHAM, Earl of
1872
Third R, xv and App 223 [2]

Descended to John Baring who presented two
of the deeds relating to Kirkstead Abbey, with
a 16th cent translation of a third, to the
British Museum in 1930 (Add Ch 67386-88)
and some Yorkshire estate papers not noticed
by the Report to Rotherham Central Library
[NRA 12413].
    A few family papers were apparently
returned to the 6th Earl after Baring's death
in 1956. The grant of Seenocliff Grange and
the letters patent creating the barony of
Effingham appeared in salerooms in 1978 and
1979. Some estate papers were bought from a
dealer by Surrey RO in 1957 [NRA 6628].

EGERTON WARBURTON, RE Esq
Arley Hall, Cheshire. 1872
Third R, xvii and App 290-92 [2]

Deposited in the John Rylands Library,
Manchester University, 1953-54 [NRA 0011].

EGLINTON AND WINTON, Earl of
Eglinton Castle, Ayrshire. 1885
Tenth R, 30-34 and App I 1-58 [10]

Deposited in the Scottish Record Office, 1952
(GD 3).
    Estate papers from 1700 onwards remain at
the Eglinton Estate Office [NRA 21021]. A
group of 19th cent Ardrossan harbour and
railway papers has been deposited in Glasgow
University Archives [NRA 21659].

EGMONT, Earl of
St James' Place London. 1879-1926
Seventh R, xiii and App 232-49 [6];
Seventeenth R, 143-53; Eighteenth R, 284-94;
Nineteenth R, 25-32; Egmont I,II;
Egmont Diary I-III [63]

Given in 1950 to the British Museum
(Add MSS 46920-47213; Add Ch 74863-929)
except the Crown Office precedent book
(Seventh R, p245a) presented to the Public
Record Office (PRO 30/26/116).

ELLACOMBE, Revd HT
Clyst St George, Devon. 1876
Fifth R, ix and App 323-29 [4]

The Bitton, Oldland and Bristol court rolls
and deeds (pp323, 326-27, 329), the copy of
the Council letter to the Marquess of Ormonde
(p327) and the 'Papers connected with
Monmouth's Rebellion' (pp327-28) were sold
to the British Museum in 1879 with other

deeds and charters (Add MSS 30999G, 31123; Add Ch 26417-513).

Some of the papers and correspondence of the Newton family (pp323-26) were included among the MSS bequeathed by TW Ellacombe to Bristol Museum and Library in 1885 and now in Bristol Central Library. Others were acquired by JL Puxley and deposited in Gloucestershire RO in 1961 with additional family papers [NRA 8754].

A further group of Newton and Creswicke family papers not noticed by the Report was also acquired by Bristol Museum and Library and transferred to Bristol RO in 1950. The Revd HT Ellacombe's correspondence and papers on campanology were bequeathed to the British Museum in 1885 (Add MSS 33202-06).

ELLESMERE see Bridgwater Trust

ELPHINSTONE, Lord
Carberry Tower, Musselburgh, Midlothian. 1884
Ninth R, xviii and App II 182-229 [8]

The Indian papers (pp207-15) were deposited in the India Office Library and Records in 1957 (MSS Eur F 87-89). The remainder were deposited with other family papers in the Scottish Record Office in 1961 (GD 156).

ELY, Bishop of
1890, 1891
Twelfth R, 44-45 and App IX 375-88 [27]

Deposited in Cambridge University Library, 1962. DM Owen, *Ely records: a handlist of the records of the bishop and archdeacon of Ely*, Cambridge, 1971.

ELY, Dean and Chapter of
1890, 1891
Twelfth R, 43-44 and App IX 389-96 [27]

Deposited in Cambridge University Library, 1970. Some groups of estate and Cathedral Grammar School papers were deposited in Cambridgeshire RO in 1961-62.

EMLY, Lord
Tervoe, co Limerick. 1881-96
Eighth R, xviii and App I 174-208 [7];
Fourteenth R, 52 and App IX 155-99 [38]

The papers and correspondence of Edmond Pery, Speaker of the Irish House of Commons, were sold to the Huntington Library, San Marino, in 1926.

Photocopies of transcripts of these and other letters are in the Public Record Office of Northern Ireland [NRA 17230]. Further Pery family papers inherited by the Earls of

Limerick were deposited in the National Library of Ireland in 1967 [NRA 8415].

ERSKINE MURRAY, Hon Mrs Isabella
Aberdona, Clackmannanshire. 1874
Fourth R, xxi-xxii and App 521-28 [3]

Sold to the National Library of Scotland with other family papers in 1939 (MSS 5070-5138).

ERSKINE MURRAY, Alexander Esq
Glasgow. 1877
Sixth R, xviii and App 709-12 [5]

The papers of the Carruthers family of Holmains were presented to the Scottish Record Office in 1961 (GD 207).

ESSEX, Custos Rotulorum and Justices of the Peace of
1885
Tenth R, 27-28 and App IV 466-513 [13]

In Essex RO. *Guide to the Essex RO* pt I, 1969.

ESSEX, Earl of
Cassiobury Park, Herts. 1914, 1917
Eighteenth R, 226-28; Various collections VII 297-350 [55]

Presented in 1922 to the British Museum (Add MSS 40625-32; Add Ch 64889-66125), and to Hertfordshire RO [NRA 7244]. The Gooderstone manorial documents (p326) were later transferred to Norfolk RO in 1953.

Other family papers and manorial documents have been deposited in Hertfordshire RO [NRA 5232, 6977] or sold to the British Library (Add MSS 60385-89; Add Ch 71032-74) at various dates since 1930.

ETON COLLEGE
1883
Ninth R, x and App I 349-58 [8]

Remain at the college in the care of the keeper of the college library and collections. MR James, *Descriptive catalogue of the MSS in the library of Eton College*, 1895. Ker, *Medieval MSS* ii, pp628-798.

EVANS, Revd D Silvan
Llanwrin, Montgomeryshire. 1899, 1902
Fifteenth R, 49; Welsh MSS II i 367-71 [48]

The four MSS noticed were presented with the Cwrtmawr MSS to the National Library of Wales.

EVERINGHAM see Herries

EWELME, Almshouse
1881, 1883
Eighth R, xiv and App I 624-32 [7];
Ninth R, App I 216-22 [8]

Deposited in the Bodleian Library, Oxford
(MS. DD. Ewelme) at various dates since 1947
[Partial list NRA 11990]. Some other accounts
of the almshouse and a letter book have been
deposited in Berkshire RO among the parish
records of Marcham.

EXETER, Bishop of
1907
Seventeenth R, 112-15; Various collections
IV 13-22 [55]

Deposited in Devon RO, 1955 [NRA 5543].

EXETER, Dean and Chapter of
1907
Seventeenth R, 115-20; Various collections
IV 23-95 [55]

Remain in the cathedral library with the
records of the archdeaconry of Exeter
[NRA 8904] and the vicars choral [NRA 8474].
LJ Lloyd and AM Erskine, *Library of Exeter
Cathedral with a short description of the
archives*, Exeter, 1974. Ker, *Medieval
MSS* ii, pp800-46.

EXETER, City of
1916, 1929
Nineteenth R, 39-41; Exeter [73]

Placed in Exeter City Library in 1930 and
now in Devon RO. SA Moore, *Calendar of
the records and muniments belonging to the
corporation of the city of Exeter*, Southwood &
Co, Exeter, 1906. *Assizes and quarter sessions
in Exeter*, Exeter, 1971. *Notes and gleanings*,
5 vols, Exeter, 1888-92. There is also a
typescript list of wills in the mayor's court
rolls, 1271-1557 [NRA 17268].

EXETER, Marquess of
Burghley House, Northants. 1877
Sixth R, xi and App 234-35 [5]

The volume containing Trevisa's translation of
Higden's Polychronicon was sold at Christie's
15 July 1959 lot 132 and bought in 1965 by the
Huntington Library, San Marino.
   Other family and estate papers remain at
Burghley House. Access through
Northamptonshire RO [Partial list NRA 6666].

EYE, Corporation of
1885
Tenth R, 26-27 and App IV 513-36 [13]

Deposited in Suffolk RO, Ipswich, 1959
[NRA 3002].

EYRE MATCHAM, Miss M
Newhouse, Salisbury, Wilts. 1909, 1917
Eighteenth R, 113-18; Various collections
VI 1-80 [55]

Bought by Lord Rosebery at Hodgson's
14 Apr 1910 lots 591-605 with other
Bubb-Dodington papers and resold in 1933
as part of his library (Sotheby's 27 June
lot 285) to the Houghton Library, Harvard
University (MSS Eng 188, 188.5F).
   Eventual recipients of other Bubb-
Dodington papers offered at these sales
include the British Library (Add MS 38019H),
the Osborn Collection, Beinecke Library,
Yale University (MS fc 83) and the Lewis
Walpole Library, Farmington, Connecticut
[NRA 22338].
   Some other Eyre Matcham family papers
were deposited in Wiltshire RO in 1978.

EYSTON, CJ Esq
Hendred House, Wantage, Berks. 1872
Third R, xxi and App 260-61 [2]

Remain at Hendred House [NRA 6534].

FARQUHARSON, Colonel James
Invercauld, Ballater, Aberdeenshire. 1874
Fourth R, xxii and App 533-35 [3]

Remain at Invercauld Castle [NRA 9958].

FAVERSHAM, Corporation of
1877
Sixth R, App 500-11 [5]

Mainly deposited in Kent AO with other
records of the corporation at various dates
since 1958. The royal charters, custumal and
first wardmote book remain at the Municipal
Offices, Faversham [NRA 7241].

FAWKES, Ayscough Esq
Farnley Hall, Yorks. 1879
Seventh R, xiv and App 509-11 [6]

Deposited in the library of the Yorkshire
Archaeological Society, Leeds in 1940.
Further family and estate papers were
deposited there in 1972 [NRA 23814].

FFARINGTON, Miss
Worden Hall, Chorley, Lancs. 1877
Sixth R, xiii and App 426-48 [5]

Deposited with other family papers in
Lancashire RO, 1940-43 [NRA 0334].

FFOLKES, Sir William Hovell Browne Bt
Hillington Hall, Norfolk. 1872
Third R, xvi and App 247-48 [2]

Dispersed by gift and sale.
   The King's Lynn register 1430-50 is now

with the corporation records at King's Lynn Town Hall.

Most of Martin Ffolkes's correspondence and scientific papers were sold at Sotheby's 27 June 1932 lots 111-26. *Notes and records of the Royal Society of London*, II, no 1, 1954, pp100-09. Eventual recipients include the Royal Society, and the Wellcome Historical Medical Library, London (MSS 1302, 2391-92).

Other family and estate papers were deposited in Norfolk RO in 1940 [Summary list NRA 4635].

FIELD, Revd Edmund
Lancing College, Sussex. 1876
Fifth R, xii and App 387-404 [4]

Deposited in Leicestershire RO in 1966 by Sir Roger Conant of Lyndon Hall [NRA 4517]. Other groups of family and estate papers have also been placed there at various dates since 1947.

FIFE, Earl
Duff House, Banffshire. 1874
Fourth R, xxiii and App 515-16 [3]

Deposited on temporary loan in the Scottish Record Office, except Spalding's History of the Troubles sold to Aberdeen University Library in 1963 and James Skene's commonplace book.

A number of other family and estate papers remain in private possession [NRA 11017, 19925].

FILMER, Sir Edmund Bt
East Sutton Park, Kent. 1872
Third R, xvi and App 246 [2]

Sold to Kent AO with other family and estate papers in 1945 [NRA 5198]. The cartulary which was missing in 1872 was presented anonymously to Kent AO in 1947. Sir Robert Filmer's Patriarcha was bought by Cambridge University Library in 1946 (Add 7078).

FINCH family
Burley-on-the-Hill, Rutland. 1879-
Seventh R, xiv and App 511-18 [6]; Eighth R, App I 640 (GH Finch) [7]; Eighteenth R, 69-84; Nineteenth R, 13-16; Twenty-Third R, 9; Twenty-Fourth R, 7; Finch I (AG Finch), Finch II (WHM Finch), Finch III, IV (JR Hanbury), V in preparation [71]

Most of the material noticed has been deposited in Leicestershire RO at various dates since 1964 with other family and estate papers including the inherited literary papers of George Savile, 1st Marquess of Halifax [NRA 9845]. Forty-three letters

noticed in Finch I and II were withdrawn for sale as autographs at Sotheby's 19 July 1966 lots 492-511 when most were bought by the Osborn Collection, Beinecke Library, Yale University. Apart from Henry Wotton's commonplace book, the legal and literary MSS listed in the Seventh R (pp514-17) are missing and thought to have been destroyed by fire in 1908.

FINGALL, Earl of
Killeen Castle, co Meath. 1885
Tenth R, 42-43 and App V 107-204 [14]

A Light to the Blind was sold to the National Library of Ireland in 1934 (MSS 476-77). Other family and estate papers were also presented to the library in 1951 (MSS 1678-88, 3640-48, 4897-4907, 8020-41, 8829-30. NRA 4115).

FITZGERALD, Sir Gerald Bt
Thurnham Hall, Lancs. 1872, 1876
Third R, xvi and App 246-47 [2];
Fifth R, App 321 [4]

Deposited in Lancashire RO in 1964 with fifty boxes of Dalton family papers [Partial list NRA 10529].

FITZGIBBON, Abraham Esq
Stanmore, Mddx. 1872
Third R, xxvi and App 431-32 [2]

The single item noticed, an anonymous history of the Desmond family, was presented to the British Museum in 1880 (Add MS 31156).

FITZHARDINGE, Lord
Berkeley Castle, Glos. 1874
Fourth R, xiv-xv and App 364-67 [3]

Remain at Berkeley Castle as the property of the Trustees of the 8th (and last) Earl of Berkeley. Access through the Gloucestershire County Archivist as their Hon Archivist. Open to advanced research scholars only. IH Jeayes, *Descriptive catalogue of the select charters and muniments at Berkeley Castle*, 1892 and supplementary list [NRA 21647]. Microfilm copies of the manorial records are held by Cambridge University Library, and of the cartulary of St Augustine's, Bristol and a few other items by the Bodleian Library, Oxford.

Some Berkeley Castle estate maps were deposited in Gloucestershire RO in 1951 [NRA 9859]. The Middlesex manorial and estate papers were deposited in the Greater London RO in 1954 [NRA 4632] and include a household book 1629-35 (cf p367).

FITZHERBERT, Sir William Bt
Tissington Hall, Derbys. 1892, 1893
Thirteenth R, 35-36 and App VI 1-185 [32]

Deposited with other family and estate
papers in Derbyshire RO, 1963
[Partial list NRA 4879].

Other papers for the family's Warsop estate
were deposited in Nottinghamshire RO in
1958 [NRA 6897].

FOLJAMBE, Rt Hon FJ
Osberton Hall, Notts. 1897, 1899
Fifteenth R, 35-39 and App V [41]

Mostly deposited in Nottinghamshire RO
with other family and estate papers at various
dates since 1962 [NRA 20442]. The royal
letters (pp123-41) remain at Osberton Hall.
Access through Nottinghamshire RO.

FOLKESTONE, Corporation of
1876
Fifth R, xvi and App 590-92 [4]

The mayor's correspondence 1463, the
single item noticed by the Report, has not
been traced since 1904. Other Folkestone
corporation and borough records 14th-20th cent
are in Folkestone Central Library
[NRA 20713].

FORBES, Lord
Castle Forbes, Keig, Aberdeenshire. 1871
Second R, xix and App 193-96 [1]

Deposited by Lord Forbes in the Scottish
Record Office in 1947 (GD 52). Some
further family papers were added in 1974
(GD 52). *Gifts and Deposits* ii, pp43-46.
Typescript inventory.

FORBES, Sir William Bt,
17th Baron Sempill
Fintray House, Aberdeenshire. 1876
Fifth R, xx and App 626-29 [4]

Deposited with other family papers in the
Scottish Record Office, 1969-71
(GD 250. NRA 10550). The papers of
Sir Andrew Mitchell were subsequently
withdrawn and sold to the British Library
in 1974 (Add MSS 58283-367;
Add Ch 75834-36). The Scottish Record
Office retains microfilms.

FORBES LEITH, James Esq
Whitehaugh, Aberdeenshire. 1871
Second R, xix and App 198-99 [1]

Mostly deposited by Lord Forbes in the
Scottish Record Office with other family
papers in 1947 (GD 52). *Gifts and Deposits* ii,
pp43-46. Typescript inventory. The earliest

baron court register and the Earl of Winton's
account book remain untraced.

Other family papers from Whitehaugh were
deposited in Aberdeen University Library
in 1958.

FORDWICH, Corporation of
1876
Fifth R, App 606-08 [4]

Deposited in Canterbury Cathedral Library
and City RO, 1956. CE Woodruff, *Inventory
and short calendar of the Fordwich municipal
documents*, typescript, 1923.

FORTESCUE, Earl
Castle Hill, South Molton, Devon. 1872
Third R, xv and App 220-21 [2]

The letters described by the Report were
deposited with other family and estate papers
in Devon RO, 1963-64 [Partial list NRA 6304].

FORTESCUE, Hon GM
Dropmore, Bucks. 1871
Second R, ix, xiii and App 49-63 [1]

The 16th and 17th cent letters noticed by the
Report were presented to the Bodleian Library,
Oxford in 1872 (MSS. Add D.109-12;
SC 29015-18) apart from Nos 103, 360, 476,
505, 508 which have not been traced.

FORTESCUE, JB Esq
Dropmore, Bucks. 1892-1928
Thirteenth R, 36-47 and App III;
Fourteenth R, 36-37 and App V; Sixteenth R,
68-79; Seventeenth R, 77-97; Eighteenth R,
144-97; Twentieth R, 5; Fortescue III-X [30]

The papers and correspondence of William
Wyndham Grenville, Baron Grenville were
bought by the British Museum in 1970
(Add MSS 58855-59494. NRA 10860).

FRANCISCAN MSS see Dublin, College
of the Irish Franciscans

FRANK, F Bacon Esq
Campsall Hall, Yorks. 1876, 1877
Fifth R, x [4]; Sixth R, xiv and App 448-65 [5]

The antiquarian collections noticed were sold
at Sotheby's 11 Aug 1942 (53 lots).

Large groups were acquired by Sheffield
Central Library (vols 1-14 described pp448-51
and the collections relating to Yorkshire
described pp459-61 passim. NRA 4883 and
Catalogue of the Arundel Castle muniments,
pp181-222, Sheffield, 1965), the Bodleian
Library, Oxford (vols 15-17, 20-21,
transcripts and other MSS pp458-64 passim.
NRA 18985) and Leeds Archives Department

(collections relating to Pontefract pp459-62 passim. NRA 5795).

The Wellcome Historical Medical Library bought Johnston's draft treatise on monarchy p462a, two of his medical notebooks p462b, the letters to his son p463, and the 15th cent Latin medical work p464a (MSS 550, 3083-85).

Other eventual recipients include the Houghton Library, Harvard University (the treatise in defence of Mary Queen of Scots and Bishop of Rosse's book p462b. fMS 1052, 1052.1), Magdalen College Library, Oxford (vol 22, p458) and the Pierpont Morgan Library, New York (Troilus and Cressida, pp464-65. M 817).

Other family and estate papers were deposited in Sheffield Central Library in 1954 or bought by it at Anderson & Garland's, Newcastle 5 Aug 1975 and 27 Apr 1976 [NRA 4883].

FRANKLAND RUSSELL ASTLEY, Mrs
Chequers Court, Bucks. 1900, 1904
Sixteenth R, 86-91; Frankland
Russell Astley [52]

Most of the papers noticed are now held by the trustees of Mrs GG Fortescue (d 1976) who inherited everything removed from Chequers Court when it was sold in 1912.

Sir John Croke's notebook (pp1-18) and some other papers were deposited in Buckinghamshire RO in 1978 by the Chequers Trustees. *Chequers catalogue*, HMSO, 1923. [NRA 16816].

Further family and estate papers have been deposited in North Yorkshire RO at various dates since 1967 [NRA 16371] and in the library of the Yorkshire Archaeological Society, Leeds [NRA 12933].

FRERE, George Edward Esq
Roydon Hall, Norfolk. 1879
Seventh R, xiv and App 518-37 [6]

The Gawdy correspondence was bought by the British Museum in 1896 (Egerton MS 2804) and the Paston correspondence in 1904 (Add MS 36988). Some other papers inherited by the Frere family from Sir John Fenn were also acquired by the British Museum as Add MSS 34888-89, 36989-91; Add Ch 53512-18.

For the dispersal of other Frere MSS not dealt with by the Report, see S De Ricci, *English collectors of books and MSS*, 1930, pp67-69.

See also: Gawdy

FREWEN, Colonel Edward
Brickwall, Northiam, Sussex. 1914, 1917
Eighteenth R, 228-29; Various collections
VII 351-59 [55]

The fifty-two deeds noticed, mainly for Northiam, were deposited with other family papers in East Sussex RO in 1965-67. *Catalogue of the Frewen Archives*, 1972 [NRA 17704].

The personal and family papers of Moreton Frewen are in the Library of Congress, Washington [NRA 22522].

GAGE, Viscount
Firle Place, Lewes, Sussex. 1872, 1928
Third R, xvi and App 223-24 [2];
Twentieth R, 5

Mostly deposited with other family papers with Sussex Archaeological Society at various dates since 1931 [NRA 9421, 12931]. Some deeds were subsequently transferred to Gloucestershire RO.

John Morton's translation of Bonaventura's Mirror of the life of Christ, including the six leaves noticed on p224, was sold at Christie's 17 Nov 1976 lot 365.

Most of General Thomas Gage's papers, with which the Report did not deal, were sold to the William L Clements Library, University of Michigan in 1930 [NRA 10567].

GALWAY, Town of
1885
Tenth R, 45-46 and App V 380-520 [14]

At University College, Galway.

GATACRE, E Lloyd Esq
Gatacre Hall, nr Bridgnorth, Salop. 1885
Tenth R, 20 and App IV 437-44 [13]

Mostly lost or destroyed. Transcripts of some have descended to EV Gatacre Esq.

Estate papers for Gatacre, Claverley and Oswestry have been deposited in Shropshire RO by Marcy Hemingway, solicitors [NRA 23113].

GAWDY family of West Harling
Walter Rye Esq, Norwich. 1885
Tenth R, 13-14 and App II [11]

Sold to the British Museum in 1889 with five other volumes of papers and correspondence (Egerton MSS 2713-22). Further Gawdy family papers, not described by the Report, are in Add MSS 14827-28, 27395-408, 48591, 56103.

The rest of Walter Rye's Norfolk antiquarian collections were bequeathed to Norwich Public Library and are now in Norfolk RO. GA Stephen, *Walter Rye. Memoir, bibliography and catalogue of his Norfolk MSS . . .* , Norwich, 1929.

GISBURNE, Hospital of Jesus
1883
Ninth R, App I 347-49 [8]

At Prior Pursglove College, Guisborough, Cleveland [NRA 3351].

GLASGOW, Corporation of
1870
First R, App 126 [1]

Now in Strathclyde Regional Archives.

GLASGOW, University of
1872
Third R, xxv and App 423-25 [2]

Remain in the Department of Special Collections, Glasgow University Library. J Young and PH Aitken, *Catalogue of the MSS in the library of the Hunterian Museum . . .*, 1908. *Brief notes on some of the important collections . . .*, typescript, 1977 [NRA 20977].

GLASGOW, Earl of
Crawford Priory, Fife, Hawkhead, Renfrewshire and Kelburn Castle, Ayrshire. 1872, 1881
Third R, xxiii and App 405-06 [2]; Eighth R, xvii and App I 304-08 [7]

The Crawford Priory charters were deposited by Lord Cochrane of Cults in the Scottish Record Office in 1953 (GD 20). *Gifts and Deposits* i, pp35-36. Typescript inventory. Some further papers were included in a deposit made by Tods, Murray and Jamieson WS of Edinburgh in 1970 (GD 237).
The Hawkhead MSS have not been seen since 1943 when they were at Crawford Priory. The Kelburn MSS remain at Kelburn Castle [NRA 10152].
Ten cartularies of the Earl of Glasgow's estates in the west of Scotland 18th-20th cent are held by McTaggart & Co, Largs [NRA 14949].

GLASTONBURY, Town of
1870
First R, App 102 [1]

The registers of proceedings of the town council temp George I are perhaps to be identified as the three corporation minute books 1786-1834 now deposited in the library of Glastonbury Antiquarian Society. The records of the parish church of St John the Baptist, apart from the early deeds, have been deposited in Somerset RO with some other borough records. The Glastonbury Abbey cartulary mentioned is British Library Add MS 22934.

GLEMHAM HALL see Guilford

GLENALMOND, Trinity College
1871
Second R, xx and App 203-05 [1]

Now kept at the Episcopal Church in Scotland Theological College, Rosebery Crescent, Edinburgh.

GLOUCESTER, Diocese of
1914, 1917
Eighteenth R, 206-11; Various collections VII 44-69 [55]

Deposited in Gloucestershire RO. IM Kirby, *Diocese of Gloucester, catalogue of the records of the bishop and archdeacons,* Gloucester, 1968.

GLOUCESTER, Dean and Chapter of
1890, 1891
Twelfth R, 47 and App IX 397-99 [27]

The early deeds, abbot's registers and books on medieval science remain in the cathedral library. SM Eward, *Catalogue of Gloucester cathedral library,* Gloucester, 1972. Ker, *Medieval MSS* ii, pp933-69.
Other capitular records have been deposited in Gloucestershire RO at various dates since 1953. IM Kirby, *Catalogue of the records of the dean and chapter . . . including the former St Peter's Abbey,* Gloucester, 1967, and typescript supplement.

GLOUCESTER, Corporation of
1890, 1891
Twelfth R, 46-47 and App IX 400-520 [27]

Deposited in Gloucestershire RO, 1974 apart from the royal charters retained at the Guildhall [NRA 21484]. WH Stevenson, *Calendar of the records of the corporation of Gloucester,* J Bellows, Gloucester, 1893, and typescript supplement.

GORDON, Hugh Mackay Esq
Abergeldie Castle, Aberdeenshire. 1877
Sixth R, xix and App 712-13 [5]

Remain at Abergeldie Castle. Not open for research.

GORDON, William Cosmo Esq
Fyvie Castle, Aberdeenshire. 1876
Fifth R, xx and App 644-46 [4]

Remain at Fyvie Castle. A list (3 vols) is held by the Scottish Record Office.

GORDON CUMMING, Sir William Bt
Gordonstoun, Elginshire. 1877
Sixth R, xix and App 681-88 [5]

Many of the autograph letters and documents noticed by the Report were sold at Sotheby's

10 Mar 1920 lots 481-92 or privately in 1965. The remainder were deposited with other family and estate papers in the National Library of Scotland in 1971 (Dep 175. NRA 10996).

GORMANSTON, Viscount
Gormanston Castle, co Meath. 1874
Fourth R, xxiv and App 573-84 [3]

The Gormanston register was bought by the National Library of Ireland in 1961 (MS 1646).

Other family papers were presented to it in 1964 (MSS 13753-65, 14231-48, 15399-408, 15997 and unsorted. NRA 9953).

GRAHAM, Sir Frederick Bt
Netherby, Cumberland. 1876-79
Fifth R, xi [4]; Sixth R, xii and App 319-22 [5]; Seventh R, xiii and App 261-428 [6]

Remain at Netherby, apart from the literary MSS noticed by the Sixth Report, pp319-20. Of these John Milton's commonplace book and the letter from Henry Lawes were sold to the British Museum in 1900 (Add MS 36354). The volume of Sir John Mandeville's Travels was sold at Sotheby's 12 Dec 1966 and resold 10 July 1972 lot 22. John Milton's Prolusion on early rising was also sold there 27 Nov 1967 lot 189. Photographic copies of the last two are now in the British Library (RP 839, 211).

Microfilm copies of most of Sir James Graham's papers 1797-1861 have been placed in the National Library of Ireland, the Bodleian Library, Oxford, Cambridge University Library and the Newberry Library, Chicago.

GRAHAM, Sir Reginald Bt
Norton Conyers, Yorks. 1876, 1877
Fifth R, xi [4]; Sixth R, xii and App 322-44 [5]

Remain at Norton Conyers.

GRAHAM family of Fintry
1909-46
Eighteenth R, 251-57; Twenty-Second R, 11; Various collections V 185-275 (Sir John James Graham) [55]; Robert Graham of Fintry [81]

In family possession [NRA 23600]. A microfilm of parts of the collection is held by the Scottish Record Office.

GRANARD, Earl of
Castle Forbes, co Longford. 1871, 1872
Second R, xx and App 210-17 [1]; Third R, xxvi and App 430-31 [2]

Remain at Castle Forbes except the transcript of the 1st Viscount Mountjoy's narrative of events in Ireland 1680-86 (Second R, pp213-15), now in the Gilbert collection, Dublin Public Libraries (MS 109).

GRANT, Sir Archibald Bt
Monymusk, Aberdeenshire. 1884
Ninth R, xix and App II 238-41 [8]

Deposited in the Scottish Record Office, 1977 (GD 345. NRA 10160). Typescript inventory.

GREAT YARMOUTH, Corporation of
1883
Ninth R, xv and App I 299-324 [8]

Deposited in Norfolk RO in 1970, apart from the royal charters and letters patent, assembly books 1550-1833 and award of Thomas Earl of Arundel 1635 which remain at Yarmouth Town Hall. *Guide to the Great Yarmouth borough records*, 1972, and typescript supplement [NRA 9311].

GRENVILLE see Fortescue, JB Esq

GREY EGERTON, Sir Philip de Malpas Bt
Malpas Hall, Cheshire. 1872
Third R, xviii and App 244-46 [2]

Destroyed in a fire at Oulton Hall, 1926. Other family and estate papers were deposited in Cheshire RO, 1970.

GRIFFITH, Miss Conway
Carreglwyd, Anglesey. 1876
Fifth R, xi-xii and App 405-23 [4]

Deposited in the National Library of Wales, 1924. *Carreglwyd deeds and documents*, typescript, 1958.

GRIMSBY, Corporation of
1895, 1896
Fourteenth R, 41-44 and App VIII 237-91 [37]

Deposited in South Humberside Area RO, Grimsby [NRA 21338].

GROVE, Commander Stanhope
Taynton, Glos. 1876
Fifth R, x and App 360-61 [4]

The five letters from General Monck and other items noticed have not been traced.

GUILFORD, Earl of
Glemham Hall, Suffolk. 1907
Seventeenth R, 122; Various collections IV,
175-90 [55]

Deposited in Suffolk RO, Ipswich in 1952
[NRA 20094], apart from some of the
St Briavels deeds (pp175-86) which were
destroyed by mildew at Glemham Hall, and
the execution warrants 1683 (pp188-89)
deposited in Kent AO in 1954.

Most of the main North family archive
from Wroxton Abbey, which the Report did
not describe, was bought by the Pilgrim Trust
in 1932 and presented to the Bodleian Library,
Oxford which has subsequently also acquired
further groups of family papers [NRA 0837].

The papers from Waldershare Park were
deposited in Kent AO in 1954 and 1976
[NRA 5392]. Those from Rougham Hall have
been deposited in Norfolk RO [NRA 4648].
Those from Kirtling Tower have become
widely dispersed by sale; many were bought
privately by the University of Kansas in 1969
and other smaller groups have also been
sold abroad.

A large group of papers mainly of
Roger North was acquired by the British
Museum in 1885 (Add MSS 32500-52).

A few letters and literary MSS which
descended to the Hon Dudleya North were
sold at Sotheby's 14 Mar 1967 lots 202-10.
(British Library microfilms RP 367, 373).

Groups of political and other
correspondence and papers of the 1st, 2nd
and 5th Earls of Guilford from Sheffield Park
were bought privately by the British Library
in 1980 and at auction in 1981 (Phillips
2 July 1981 lots 263, 298, 300). Fifty-eight
volumes of confidential army reports 1770-82
from the library of the 2nd Earl were acquired
by the William L Clements Library,
University of Michigan, in 1948.

GUNNING, Sir Henry Bt
Horton, Northants. 1872
Third R, xviii and App 248-50 [2]

The official papers of Walter Titley and of
Robert Gunning were bought by the
British Museum in 1888 (Egerton MSS
2680-2706).

Some estate papers 18th-19th cent were
deposited in Northamptonshire RO in 1957.

GURNEY, John Henry Esq
Keswick Hall, Norfolk. 1890, 1891
Twelfth R, 39-40 and App IX 116-64 [27]

Sold at Sotheby's 30 Mar 1936 lots 72-213.
The seventeen lots bought by A de Coppet
were resold at Sotheby's 4 July 1955 and
2 Apr 1957.

The fourteen volumes of Sir Henry
Spelman's miscellanea were broken up and
their contents have become widely dispersed.

Only about one half can now be traced.
Eventual recipients of parts include the
Bodleian Library, Oxford (MSS. Dugdale 51;
Eng.hist.c.241, 242, 272; Eng.misc.d.247),
the John Rylands Library, Manchester
University (Eng MSS 874, 880), Norfolk RO
(MSS 7197, 7198, T139F), Suffolk RO
(HD 695, 802/1), the British Library
(Egerton MSS 3138, 3139B), the Osborn
Collection, Beinecke Library, Yale University,
and other American libraries.

The Leges Angliae (pp116-22) is now
Rylands Library Lat MS 420. John Walker's
commonplace book (p123), Sir Richard
Hutton's journals (pp125-27) and Lydgate's
Destruction of Thebes (p164) with two
treatises on astrology and geometry are in
Cambridge University Library (Add 6860-68).
Sir George Downing's journal (pp163-64) is at
Downing College, Cambridge. The Macro
Mystery Plays are in the Folger Library,
Washington (MS. V.a. 354). The Blackborough
chartulary (p122) is British Library
Egerton MS 3137.

Some other family papers have been
deposited in Norfolk RO [NRA 5955, 15293].

GUTHRIE, John Esq
Guthrie Castle, Angus. 1871
Second R, xix and App 197-98 [1]

Deposited with other family papers in the
Scottish Record Office, 1964-65
(GD 188. NRA 8402).

GWYSANEY see Davies Cooke

HAILSTONE, Edward Esq
Walton Hall, Wakefield, Yorks. 1881
Eighth R, xiii-xiv and App I 636-37 [7]

Mostly bequeathed to York Minster Library
as the Hailstone collection. Some of the bound
volumes listed on p636 section (a) were
included in the sale of Hailstone's library at
Sotheby's 23 Apr 1891.

HALIDAY, Charles Esq
Monkstown, nr Dublin, d.1866
Thirteenth R, 56; Fifteenth R, 45-46 and
App III [40], 1892-99

The single volume described remains in the
Royal Irish Academy, Dublin (MS 24.F.17).

HAMILTON, Duke of
Hamilton Palace, Lanarkshire. 1870-1938
First R, xii and App 112-14 [1]; Eleventh R,
38-42 and App VI; Twenty-First R, 13;
Supplementary Report [21]

Mostly still in family possession at
Lennoxlove [NRA 10979].

Some bound volumes noticed in the First Report were among the MSS sold to the Royal Library, Berlin in 1882. See S De Ricci, *English collectors of books and MSS*, 1930, pp86-87. The twelve volumes relating to affairs between England and Scotland temp James V were subsequently purchased for the British Museum in 1886 (Add MSS 32646-57). Twenty-nine further MSS bought for the Museum in 1887 included the Gesta Cnutonis (Add MS 33241), the Furness Abbey coucher book vol ii (Add MS 33244), Burnet's Memoirs (Add MS 33259) and Cleland's transcripts relating to Mary Queen of Scots (Add MS 33256).

Some family correspondence and papers were presented to the National Library of Scotland in 1931 by the trustees of the late Sir William Fraser, compiler of Eleventh R, App VI (MSS 1031-32). The papers of William Beckford (Supplementary Report p vii. NRA 22980) were sold at Sotheby's 6 July 1977, lot 272 to BH Blackwell Ltd of Oxford.

HAMILTON, Miss

Cochno House, Dunbartonshire. 1881
Eighth R, xvii and App I 308-10 [7]

Deposited in Strathclyde Regional Archives, 1979 [NRA 14829].

HARE, Sir Thomas Bt

Stow Hall, Stow Bardolph, Norfolk. 1872
Third R, xvi and App 250-52 [2]

Mostly deposited with Norfolk Record Society in 1942 and now in Norfolk RO. The Bolingbroke correspondence (p252) was sold at Sotheby's 3 June 1946 lots 404-10 and has not been traced, apart from some items in New York Public Library (*National union catalog* MS 71-337). The forged charter of William I to Ramsey Abbey (p250) was presented to the British Museum in 1947 (Add Ch 74436). The British Museum also acquired some other Bolingbroke correspondence not listed by the Report in 1958 (Add MSS 49970-71).

HARE, Theodore J Esq

Borden Wood, Sussex. 1895, 1896
Fourteenth R, 37-38 and App IX 200-66 [38]

In private possession.

HARFORD, Mrs

Holme Hall, Market Weighton, Yorks.
1903, 1904
Sixteenth R, 108; Various collections
II 348-66 [55]

A View of the Trained Bands (p349), the correspondence and papers of the

Commissioners of Sewers for the East Riding 1663-65 (p364) and the letter of the Lords Commissioners for the Subsidy (p365) are among the papers from Holme Hall presented by Mrs Harford to the British Museum between 1921 and 1925 (Add MSS 40132-37, 41168, 41178 O; Add Ch 63734-38, 66599-601, 66608).

The other documents noticed, consisting chiefly of letters addressed to Marmaduke Lord Langdale, were sold at Sotheby's 18 July 1955 lots 514-28 and are now dispersed.

Some further papers of the Langdale family of Holme were deposited in the former East Riding RO in 1955 and moved to the Brynmor Jones Library, Hull University in 1974 [NRA 6488].

HARTLAND, Parish of

1874, 1876
Fourth R, xix and App 428-29 [3]; Fifth R, xvi-xvii and App 571-75 [4]

Deposited in Devon RO, 1963. ID Thornley, *Calendar of Hartland parish documents*, typescript, 1924-30 [NRA Devon parish reports].

HARVEY, John Esq

Ickwell Bury, Beds and Finningley Park, Yorks. 1870, 1871
First R, x and App 62-63;
Second R, xv-xvi and App 89-91 [1]

Most of the MSS described in the First Report were contained in forty-five mixed volumes of printed tracts and MSS that were sold at Sotheby's 19 June 1922 lots 520-64. One volume in which some of them are bound is now in the Pierpont Morgan Library, New York (MA 1201), another is in the William L Clements Library, University of Michigan (HS Smith collection). A third is in the possession of Dr BE Jeul-Jensen at Oxford.

The seven bound volumes of MS tracts etc noticed by the Second Report are thought to have been destroyed in a fire at Ickwell Bury in 1937.

The family and estate papers deposited in Bedfordshire RO in 1947 [NRA 0682] include an Italian diary 1709-14 (cf p91).

HASTINGS, Corporation of

1892
Thirteenth R, 50 and App IV 354-64 [31]

In the custody of Hastings Borough Council. Access through the curator, Hastings Museum and Art Gallery [NRA 5876].

HASTINGS, Reginald Rawdon Esq
Ashby de la Zouch, Leics. d.1915
Twentieth R, 5; Twenty-First R, 12-13;
Hastings I-IV [78], 1928-47

Sold to Henry E Huntington in 1926 with
many other estate papers (Maggs Bros
Cat. 1926). Now in the Huntington Library,
San Marino [NRA 10029].

HATFIELD see Salisbury, Marquess of

HATHERTON, Lord
Teddesley Hall, Staffs. 1876
Fifth R, vii-viii and App 294-99 [4]

Mostly deposited in Staffordshire RO at
various dates since 1953, with other
¡Littleton and Persehouse family papers
ncluding the correspondence and journals of
the 1st-3rd Barons Hatherton [NRA 4022].
The Anne Boleyn letter (p296) is in the
Pierpont Morgan Library, New York. Most
of the other autograph letters (pp295-96) have
not been traced.

HATTON see Winchilsea and Nottingham

HAVOD see Banks; Williams, Revd R Peris

HAY, Robert Mordaunt Esq
Duns Castle, Berwickshire. 1909, 1917
Eighteenth R, 242-47; Various collections
V 1-71 [55]

Remain at Duns Castle [NRA 10165].
Some other MSS from Duns Castle were
sold at Christie's 28 Apr 1966 lot 162
(Lauder Brown Devotions, now National
Library of Scotland MS 9998), 30 Nov 1966
lots 97-110 and 28 June 1972 lot 50
(Scottish National Covenant).

HEATHCOTE, JM Esq
Conington Castle, Hunts. 1899, 1904
Sixteenth R, 62-68; Heathcote
(Fanshawe MSS) [50]

Sold at Sotheby's 18 Dec 1912 lots 124-210.
Eleven lots comprising about half the papers
listed and including the bulk of those of
Sir Richard Fanshawe were bought by
Captain BT Fanshawe and subsequently
presented with other family papers to the
Valence Library, Dagenham between 1961 and
1963. The remainder have not been traced
although individual items have reappeared
from time to time in the salerooms,
eg Sotheby's 4 July 1944 lot 769, 22 June 1955
lot 768.
　　Among other family papers not noticed by
the Report an original of Lady Fanshawe's
memoirs was bought by the British Museum

in 1924 (Add MS 41161). Some further papers
of Sir Richard Fanshawe were deposited in
Leicestershire RO in 1957. A small group of
miscellaneous Fanshawe family papers was
bought by Hertfordshire RO in 1967
[NRA 18339].

HEIDELBERG, University Library
1870
First R, xi and App 132 [1]

Remain in the university library.

HELMINGHAM see Tollemache

HENGWRT see Wynne

HEREFORD, Corporation of
1892
Thirteenth R, 50-51 and App IV 283-353 [31]

Mostly deposited in Hereford City Library,
1965-68, and now in Hereford and
Worcester RO, Hereford [NRA 12489]. The
royal charters remain with the chief executive
and town clerk of Hereford City Council.
EM Jancey, *The royal charters of the city of
Hereford*, 1973.

HERRIES, Lord
Everingham Park, Yorks. 1870
First R, xi and App 45-46 [1]

Most of the historical papers noticed are
among those of the Maxwell-Constable
family from Everingham that were
deposited successively by the 16th Duke of
Norfolk at Ampleforth Abbey 1954-60 and
the East Riding RO 1960-74, and are now in
the Brynmor Jones Library, Hull University
[NRA 11211].
　　Some of the medieval MSS were sold
through WH Robinson, Newcastle (*Cat.* 12)
in 1925, and have been dispersed. The Drax
cartulary is now Bodleian Library
MS. Top.Yorks.c.72. The Passionarium
G. De Lacy is Newcastle University Library
MS 1. Those retained in family possession
have been moved to Arundel Castle.

HERTFORD, Corporation of
1895
Fourteenth R, App VIII 158-64 [37]

Deposited in Hertfordshire RO, 1974.
Typescript catalogue.

HERTFORD, Marquess of
1874
Fourth R, xiii and App 251-54 [3]

The registers of Goa (p252) and the pedigree of Sir John Conway (p254) are among the Seymour-Conway family papers deposited in Warwickshire RO at various dates since 1936 [NRA 8482]. The letter about Hudson's Bay was sold at Sotheby's 10 Nov 1959 lot 210. The MS Judicature in Parliament was sold at Sotheby's 7 Dec 1959 lot 256 and is now in Birmingham Reference Library. The volume of Daniel Rogers's latin poems, sold at Sotheby's 23 June 1969 lot 169, is now MS HM 31188 in the Huntington Library, San Marino.

Some other papers of the Seymour-Conway family which descended to Sir Richard Wallace and afterwards to Sir John Murray Scott were bought by the British Museum in 1942 (Egerton MSS 3257-65). Some further Conway family papers were sold at Sotheby's 26 Oct 1970 lot 375 and are now in the Taylor collection, Princeton University Library.

HEWITT, Thomas Esq
Cork. 1870
First R, xii and App 129 [1]

Untraced except for the Cork shrievalty papers, now in University College, Cork (MS U 55).

HIGH WYCOMBE, Borough of
1876
Fifth R, xvii and App 554-65 [4]

Kept in Wycombe District Council strongroom in the custody of the curator of Wycombe Chair and Local History Museum.

HIGHAM FERRERS, Corporation of
1890, 1891
Twelfth R, 47-48 and App IX 530-37 [27]

Deposited in Northamptonshire RO in 1944, except for the corporation acts and royal charters (pp535-36) which remain at Higham Ferrers Town Hall and some accounts and presentments 1573-1642 from the small deal box (p537) now held by solicitors.

HILL, Revd TS
Thorington Rectory, Suffolk. 1885
Tenth R, 23 and App IV 451-57 [13]

The Blythburgh cartulary, terrier and rental (Nos I, IV, V) were bought by the British Museum in 1922 and 1954 (Add MSS 40725, 48381-82). The documents relating to Wenhaston (Nos II, III) were presented to the parish chest in 1893 and deposited with other parish records in Suffolk RO, Ipswich in 1962.

HODGKIN, J Eliot Esq
Richmond, Surrey. 1897, 1899
Fifteenth R, 41-42 and App II [39]

Dispersed by auction at Sotheby's between 22 Apr and 19 May 1914, when the British Museum's purchases (Add MSS 38846-64, 40166, 57309) included Sir Bernard Gascoigne's letter book (pp125-53) and many of the Pepys, Danby and Jacobite papers. The D'Eon papers (pp352-68) are now in the Brotherton Library, Leeds University. The remainder have become widely scattered and much cannot now be traced.

HOLKHAM see Leicester, Earl of

HOME, Earl of
The Hirsel, Coldstream, Berwickshire.
1890, 1891
Twelfth R, 51 and App VIII 76-185 [26]

Remain at the Hirsel [NRA 10169]. The Scottish Record Office holds some other miscellaneous writs (GD 1/180).

HOME OF RENTON see Stirling

HOOD, Sir Alexander Fuller Acland, 1st Baron St Audries
St Audries, Watchet, Somerset. 1876, 1877
Fifth R, xi [4]; Sixth R, xii-xiii and App 344-52 [5]

Mostly deposited with other family and estate papers in Somerset RO, 1972-73 [NRA 5299]. A few of the medieval MSS were sold privately. Nicholas Trivet's translation of the French chronicle (pp344-45) is now in the Houghton Library, Harvard University (fMS Eng 938). Wycliffe's translation of the Bible (p344) is in the Scheide collection, Princeton University Library.

Some other family papers were deposited in East Sussex RO in 1955 [NRA 5298].

HOPE JOHNSTONE, JJ Esq
Raehills, Dumfriesshire. 1897, 1899
Fifteenth R, 45 and App IX [46]

Remain at Raehills [NRA 12630].

HOPKINSON, Revd Francis
Malvern Wells, Worcs. 1872
Third R, xvi and App 261-67 [2]

Mostly untraced. Five of the items noticed by the Report were sold at Sotheby's 3 June 1905 lots 722-33 with other material from the collection. A few more were included in a sale of books there 17 July 1916, among them the Devyse to entertain Her Majesty

1602 (p264) now in the Folger Library, Washington. A bound volume containing sixty-five documents from the collection, mostly associated with William Cecil, Lord Burghley, and including fifteen of the items noticed by the Report, is in the possession of the Marquess of Exeter (Burghley House muniments 51/1. Access through Northamptonshire RO. NRA 6666).

HOSKINS, Dr Samuel Elliott
Guernsey. 1871
Second R, xiii and App 158-65 [1]

The Civil War journal of Jean Chevalier is now owned by the Société Jersiaise, St Helier, Jersey for whom it was edited, 1906-14, by JA Messervy.

HOTHFIELD, Lord
Chesterfield Gardens, London W. 1887, 1888
Eleventh R, 23 and App VII 81-90 [22]

Deposited in Cumbria RO, Kendal with papers from Appleby Castle at various dates since 1962. Partial list, 1916 [NRA 12905].

Other estate papers of the Clifford and Tufton families from Skipton Castle also listed in 1916 [NRA 12905] were deposited in the library of the Yorkshire Archaeological Society, Leeds in 1955 and 1978. Their Kent estate papers have been deposited in Kent AO at various dates since 1954 [NRA 4391].

HOUSE OF LORDS
1870-94
First R, xi-xii and App 1-10; Second R, ix and App 106-09 [1]; Third R, xi and App 1-36 [2]; Fourth R, x-xi and App 1-170 [3]; Fifth R, vi and App 1-134 [4]; Sixth R, vii-x and App 1-221 [5]; Seventh R, vii-xiii and App 1-182 [6]; Eighth R, viii-x and App I 101-74 [7]; Ninth R, v-viii and App II 1-125 [8]; Eleventh R, 10-11 and App II; Twelfth R, 10-12 and App VI; Thirteenth R, 10-13 and App V; Fourteenth R, 4-6 and App VI [17]

Remain in the House of Lords Record Office. For the years after 1693 publication has been continued as House of Lords Papers, see *Government Publications Sectional List 24 (British National Archives)*.

HULTON, WWB Esq
Hulton Park, Lancs. 1890, 1891
Twelfth R, 40 and App IX 165-78 [27]

Mostly deposited in Lancashire RO with other family papers in 1943 [NRA 0214]. The collection of letters from Robert Devereux, 2nd Earl of Essex to Queen Elizabeth I etc (pp166-74) was deposited in the British Museum in 1945 (MS Loan 23), which also acquired further

papers of William Jessop in 1946 (Add MSS 46188-91; Add Ch 71765-97).

HUME CAMPBELL, Sir Hugh Bt
Marchmont House, Berwickshire. 1894
Fourteenth R, 47-49 and App III 56-173 [34]

Deposited with other family papers in the Scottish Record Office at various dates since 1930 (GD 158. NRA 8151).

Some 19th cent estate papers have been deposited in Reading University Library [NRA 13862].

HUNSTANTON, Vicarage of
1883
Ninth R, App I 358 [8]

Remain with the incumbent, Old Hunstanton. Transcripts of the two early parish registers 1538-1754 are held by Norfolk and Norwich Archaeological Society.

HUNTLY, Marquess of
Aboyne Castle, Aberdeenshire. 1871
Second R, xvii and App 180 [1]

Thirty-eight boxes of Aboyne writs 1561-1859 have been deposited in the Scottish Record Office at various dates since 1957 (GD 181; 1/584). Some additional Huntly papers were bought by it in 1975 (GD 312).

HYTHE, Corporation of
1874
Fourth R, xviii and App 429-39 [3]

Remain at the Municipal Offices in the care of the honorary archivist. HD Dale and C Chidell, *Catalogue of documents belonging to the corporation of Hythe 11th-20th centuries*, Hythe, 1937.

See also: Mackeson

HYTHE, Hospital of St Bartholomew
1877
Sixth R, App 511-22 [5]

Remain in the care of the clerk to the trustees of the hospitals of St Bartholomew and St John, 86 High St, Hythe, Kent.

INGILBY, Sir Henry Bt
Ripley Castle, Yorks. 1876, 1877
Fifth R, x-xi [4]; Sixth R, xiii and App 352-95 [5]

Mostly dispersed by auction at Sotheby's 21 Oct 1920 (44 items, lots 1-183 passim) or by private sales. The residue has been deposited with other family papers in Leeds Archives Department [NRA 11614] apart from the Mountgrace Priory charter (p360b) which remains at Ripley Castle.

Eventual recipients of the material sold include the British Library (Add MSS 40006-11A,B, 46203, 62129-30, 62132; Add Ch 62747-58; Egerton MS 2864), Leeds Archives Department (Henry of Knaresborough's latin sermons bought with the Vyner papers in 1981, NRA 6160), the Bodleian Library (letters to Ralph Palmer pp390–95: MSS. Eng. lett. c. 438, d. 409), Canterbury Cathedral and City RO (William Brewyn's account of his pilgrimage to Rome), the John Rylands Library, Manchester University (the latin sermons p357a: Lat MS 365. Vol Q-Z of the Fountains Abbey coucher book noted as lost on p358a: Lat MS 224) and a number of American institutions including the Huntington Library, San Marino (the Aurea Legenda and the Psalms of David) and Princeton University Library (Higden's Polychronicon and two other items).

INNER TEMPLE
1871-88
Second R, xv and App 151-56 [1]; Eleventh R, 36-38 and App VII 227-308 [22]

Remain in the Inner Temple Library. *Catalogue of MSS in the library of the Honourable Society of the Inner Temple*, ed J Conway Davies, 3 vols, 1972.

IPSWICH, Corporation of
1883
Ninth R, xi-xiii and App I 222-62 [8]

Deposited in Suffolk RO, Ipswich in 1950 with other records [Partial list NRA 3819].

IRELAND, Jesuit Archives
1885
Tenth R, 44-45 and App V 340-79 [14]

With the archivist of the Irish Province of the Society of Jesus, 35 Lower Leeson St, Dublin 2.

IRVINE, Alexander Forbes Esq
Drum Castle, Aberdeenshire. 1871
Second R, xix and App 198 [1]

Remain with other family papers at Drum Castle as the property of the National Trust for Scotland [NRA 20772]. Photocopies are held by the Scottish Record Office (RH1/2/748-54) which has also some stray family letters 1763-1819 bought at Sotheby's 6 June 1978 (GD 1/865; typescript inventory).

ISHAM, Sir Charles Bt
Lamport Hall, Northants. 1872
Third R, xviii and App 252-54 [2]

Many of the volumes listed under the heading Heraldry and Genealogy (pp252-53) were sold at Sotheby's 17 June 1904 lots 43-347 passim. Of these the Tewkesbury Abbey register is now British Library Add MS 36985 and the Conference of Weightes is in the Folger Library, Washington. Other MS volumes that appear to have been sold privately or in unidentified sales include William Smith's Abuses committed by painters and Richard Barnfield's poems (p253) which were also acquired 1904-05 by the Folger Library.

The remainder are now among the Isham family papers deposited in Northamptonshire RO [NRA 4601].

JAMES, Revd John see Salisbury,
Dean and Chapter of

JAMIESON, GA see Breadalbane

JERSEY, Earl of
Osterley Park, Mddx. 1881
Eighth R, xi and App I 92-101 [7]

Most of the twenty-five volumes calendared by the Report were dispersed by sale at Sotheby's 6 May 1885 and 30 May 1949. Eventual recipients include London University Library (No 1), the British Library (Nos 2, 3, 5, 8: Add MSS 32469-72), the Bodleian Library, Oxford (No 4: MS. Add.c.273), the Library of Congress, Washington (No 20), Princeton University Library (No 22) and the John Rylands Library, Manchester University (No 23).

No 16 is with the papers of the Child-Villiers family deposited in the Greater London RO at various dates since 1952 [NRA 0935].

Other family and estate papers have been deposited in Kent AO [NRA 4811], Warwickshire RO and Oxfordshire RO.

JERVOISE, FHT Esq
Herriard Park, Hants. 1907
Seventeenth R, 122; Various collections IV 140-74 [55]

Deposited with other family papers in Hampshire RO, 1969 [NRA 18628].

KENDAL, Corporation of
1885
Tenth R, 16 and App IV 299-318 [13]

Deposited in Cumbria RO, Kendal in 1976 apart from the royal charters (p299) and book of record (pp310-18) retained by the town clerk.

KENNEDY ERSKINE, AJWH Esq
Dun House, Angus. 1876
Fifth R, xxi and App 633-44 [4]

Deposited in the Scottish Record Office in
1962 (GD 123) except the volume of royal
and other letters 16th-17th cent addressed
mainly to John Erskine, Superintendent of
Angus which is thought to remain at
Dun House [NRA 8400].

KENYON, Lord
Gredington Hall, Flints. 1894, 1896
Fourteenth R, 31-36 and App IV [35]

Remain at Gredington.
　Large numbers of other family papers
were deposited in Lancashire RO in 1951
[NRA 19460]. The papers of Lloyd Kenyon
as a JP in Maelor 1726-72 were deposited in
Clwyd RO, Hawarden in 1967 [NRA 12705].
Inherited papers of the Tyrell family of
Boreham were deposited in Essex RO in 1940
[NRA 8507].

KETTON, RW Esq
Felbrigg Hall, Norfolk. 1890, 1891
Twelfth R, 40-42 and App IX 179-226 [27]

The 15th cent transcript of Paston family
letters (pp179-82) and the letters to
William Windham (pp225-26) were given to
the British Museum in 1937 and 1962
(Add MSS 45099, 50851). The other papers
noticed have been deposited in or bequeathed
to Norfolk RO with other family papers at
various dates since 1954 [NRA 4644].

KILKENNY, Corporation of
1870, 1871
First R, App 129-30; Second R, xxi and
App 257-62 [1]

The MSS noticed by the First Report
remained in the custody of the town clerk at
Kilkenny in 1961. Rothe's register, described
by the Second Report, is now in Dublin
Public Libraries (MSS 105-06).

KILMOREY, Earl of
Shavington Hall, Market Drayton, Salop. 1885
Tenth R, 17-18 and App IV, 358-74 [13]

Mostly deposited with other family deeds and
papers in Shropshire RO either by
Lord Kilmorey in 1947 or by Lt-Colonel
A Heywood-Lonsdale (whose grandfather
bought the Shavington estate in 1885) in
1959. The present whereabouts of the two
volumes of transcripts of miscellaneous
documents relating to Salop and Cheshire
(pp365-72) and the inventory roll 1631 of the
goods of Robert Viscount Kilmorey (p374) is
not known. The Report is supplemented by

HD Harrod, *Muniments of Shavington*,
Shrewsbury, 1891.

KING, Lt-Colonel William Ross
Tertowie House, Kinnellar, Aberdeenshire.
1872
Third R, xvii and App 416 [2]

The papers of William King, archbishop of
Dublin, were deposited in Aberdeen
University Library in 1978 with other
King and Innes family papers
[Summary list NRA 22349].

KING'S LYNN, Corporation of
1887
Eleventh R, 33-36 and App III 145-247 [18]

Remain at the town hall, in the care of
Norfolk RO [NRA 3008].

KINGSMILL, Andrew Esq
Sydmonton Court, Hants. 1899
Fifteenth R, App X 173-74 [47]

Remain in family possession. Microfilm copies
are held at Hampshire RO [NRA 10665].

**KINGSTON UPON THAMES,
Corporation of**
1872
Third R, xx and App 331-33 [2]

Now in Surrey RO. *Guide to the Kingston
borough archives*, 1971 and typescript
supplement [NRA 3009].

KINNAIRD, Lord
Rossie Priory, Perthshire. 1876
Fifth R, xx and App 620-21 [4]

Deposited in the Scottish Record Office,
1949 (GD 48). *Gifts and Deposits* ii, pp34-35.
Typescript inventory.
　Other family papers remain at Rossie Priory
[NRA 20216].

KINNOULL, Earl of
Dupplin Castle, Perthshire. 1874
Fourth R, xxiii and App 514-15 [3]

The charters and other material noticed remain
in family possession [NRA 10998], apart from
the copy of Boece's Cronikillis of Scotland
which was sold at Sotheby's 7 Nov 1911
with other items from Dupplin Castle and is
now in the Pierpont Morgan Library,
New York (M 527).

KIRKCUDBRIGHT, Burgh of
1874
Fourth R, xxiii and App 538-39 [3]

Remain in the council offices at
Kirkcudbright in the custody of the
chief executive of Stewartry District Council.

KNIGHTLEY, Sir Rainald Bt
Fawsley Park, Northants. 1872
Third R, xix and App 254-55 [2]

The volume of parliamentary journals for
1625 and 1640 which the Report describes
has not been seen since 1936 when it remained
at Fawsley Park. The Commons journal for
1625 was printed by SR Gardiner,
Debates in the House of Commons in 1625,
Camden Society, new ser vi, 1873.

Other Knightley family and estate papers
were deposited with Northamptonshire
Record Society at various dates after 1921
and are now in Northamptonshire RO. A few
Knightley-Sebright family papers were also
transferred there from Hertfordshire RO in
1936 [NRA 7251]. Lady Louisa Knightley's
autograph collection was presented to the
British Museum in 1946 (Add MSS 46356-61).

KNOLE see Sackville

KNOX, Captain Howard Vicente
1909, 1917
Eighteenth R, 118-27; Various collections VI
81-296, 440-49 [55]

Sold with 120 further letters to the
William L Clements Library, University of
Michigan in 1931.

**KYLE, Dr James Francis, Bishop of
Germanicia**
Buckie and Preshome, Banffshire. 1870
First R, xi and App 120 [1]

Most of the material noticed was deposited in
Blairs College, Aberdeen at various dates
after 1870 and transferred to the Scottish
Catholic Archives, Columba House,
Edinburgh in 1958 [Partial list NRA 7865].
A few letters of Mary Queen of Scots and the
Glasgow protocol book 1499-1513 were
retained by the college but subsequently
deposited with the remainder of its library in
the National Library of Scotland in 1974-75
[NRA 20740]. See further D McRoberts,
'The Scottish Catholic Archives, 1560-1978',
Innes Review, xxviii, 1977, pp59-128.

LAING MSS see Edinburgh, University of

LAMBETH PALACE
1877
Sixth R, xiv and App 522-24 [5]

The contents of the fifty bags of parchment
and paper rolls noticed by the Report have
now mostly been redistributed between the
Carte Antique et Miscellanee (MSS 889-901)
and the Estate Document Collection there.
DM Owen, *Catalogue of Lambeth MSS 889 to
901*, 1968, and J Sayers, *Estate documents at
Lambeth Palace Library*, 1965. The roll
endorsed with seven French poems is now
MS 1681 (formerly Misc Rolls 1435),
see Ker, *Medieval MSS* i, p114.

LAMINGTON see Cochrane

LANSDOWNE, Marquess of
Lansdowne House, London and Bowood,
Calne, Wilts. 1871-77
Second R, viii [1]; Third R, xii and
App 125-47 [2];
Fourth R, xii [3]; Fifth R, vii and
App 215-60 [4]; Sixth R, xi and
App 235-43 [5]

Vols 1-99, 101-25, 127-55, 161-68 were
bought in 1921 by William L Clements and
are now in the William L Clements Library,
University of Michigan, with other papers of
the 1st Marquess of Lansdowne bought
privately in 1929 or at Sotheby's 23 Apr 1934
lots 383-448.

The ancient MSS (Vols 169-200) and
Vol 201 were sold in 1876 to the British
Museum (Add MSS 30190-237) which in
1934 also acquired forty letters addressed to
Henry Cromwell (Sixth R, pp238, 242:
Add MS 43724).

Vol 126 has not been seen since 1921.
Vols 100, 156-60, the unbound correspondence
and some, if not all, of vols 201B-210 remain
at Bowood, but are not open for research.

LAUDERDALE, Earl of
Thirlestane Castle, Lauder, Berwickshire. 1876
Fifth R, xix-xx and App 610-13 [4]

Remain at Thirlestane Castle [NRA 10211].

LAUNCESTON, Corporation of
1877
Sixth R, App 524-26 [5]

Remain at Launceston Town Hall in the
custody of the clerk of the council
[NRA 23454].

LAWSON, Sir John Bt
Brough Hall, Yorks. 1872-76
Third R, xvi and App 255-56 [2]; Fourth R,
xv and App 367-68 [3]; Fifth R, viii and
App 305-07 [4]

The medieval MS books were sold at
Sotheby's 23 July 1906. The Life of
St Cuthbert is now British Library
Add MS 39943. The York Manual is MS 1,
in the Harry Elkins Widener collection,
Houghton Library, Harvard University.
The psalter of Robert Blakeney is
MS. Lat.liturg.g.8 in the Bodleian Library,
Oxford. The recusant and Jacobite documents
(Third R, p255) have not been traced. The
Neasham Priory deeds and the Memorials of
the church of Durham are among the family
papers deposited in North Yorkshire RO in
1973 [NRA 20995].

LECHMERE, Sir Edward Bt
Rhydd Court, Upton on Severn, Worcs. 1876
Fifth R, viii and App 299-304 [4]

Mostly deposited in Hereford and
Worcester RO, Worcester with other family
and estate papers in 1953 [NRA 3992].
Some related Bellomont papers were also
deposited there in 1964 [NRA 10423].

LECONFIELD, Lord
Petworth House, Sussex. 1876, 1878
Fifth R, xi [4]; Sixth R, xii and
App 287-319 [5]

Fifty-seven of the MSS noticed by the
Reports were sold at Sotheby's 23 Apr 1928.
The Ely Priory register (pp289-300) was
acquired with six others for the British Museum
(Add MSS 41612-17, 41667G). The 14th cent
volume of treaties (pp301-03) is now in the
John Rylands Library, Manchester University
(Lat MS 404). Other eventual recipients
include the National Maritime Museum (7),
Clifton College Science Library, Bristol (3),
the Wellcome Historical Medical Library,
London (1), Blackburn Museum and Art
Gallery (1) and a number of American
libraries. The National Library of Ireland
purchased papers of the 1st Earl of Orrery
(lot 20) not listed in the Reports, and has
microfilm copies of those noticed pp316-18.

The rest of the material listed including the
Harriot papers (p319) and the papers of the
2nd Earl of Bristol (pp315-16) remains at
Petworth House. Access through West
Sussex RO. For further family and estate
papers there see FW Steer and others,
Petworth House archives, 2 vols, 1968, 1979.
For the papers at Cockermouth now in the
custody of Cumbria RO, Carlisle
see NRA 12202. Thirty-one bundles of papers
of the 2nd Earl of Egremont were deposited
in the Public Record Office in 1947
(PRO 30/47. NRA 8663). The Irish estate

papers were deposited in the Public Record
Office of Northern Ireland in 1976.

LEE, JH Esq
Redbrook House, Whitchurch, Salop. 1872
Third R, xvii and App 267-68 [2]

The year books and other legal papers
described, remained in family possession in
1941. No subsequent information is available.

LEEDS, Duke of
Hornby Castle, Yorks. 1887, 1888
Eleventh R, 11-13 and App VII 1-58 [22]

Most of the papers listed by the Report were
deposited on loan in the British Museum after
the death of the 10th Duke in 1927 and
subsequently purchased by it in 1947
(Egerton MSS 3324-3508; Egerton
Ch 2290-2300). The MS treatise by
Dean Colet (p40) and the Roman de la Rose
(p58) remain deposited there as
MS Loan 55/1-2.

The twenty-five volumes of accounts etc
of Lord Danby as Lord High Treasurer
(pp39-40) were sold to the Public Record
Office in 1929 (PRO 30/32. NRA 8655).
Thirteen items of American interest
(pp10, 13, 14, 19, 32, 38, 39, 45, 48) were sold
at Sotheby's 16 Dec 1946 lots 369-74.

The deeds (pp56-58) were deposited with
other family papers in the library of the
Yorkshire Archaeological Society, Leeds
[NRA 12923], Buckinghamshire
Archaeological Society Museum and
Cornwall RO.

From earlier sales of family papers at
Sotheby's 11 July 1868 and 5 Apr 1869
(A Browning, *Thomas Osborne* ii, 1944,
pp3-4) the British Museum acquired the
contents of Add MSS 27914-18, 28040-95,
28570, 38849 ff 115-327 (via the JE Hodgkin
collection), 39757 ff 40-105 (via the
Morrison collection).

A few miscellaneous MSS not listed by the
Report were included in the sale of books
from Hornby Castle at Sotheby's 2 June 1930.

See also: Hodgkin; Lindsey; Morrison;
Webster

LE FLEMING, SH Esq
Rydal Hall, Ambleside, Westmorland. 1890
Twelfth R, 38-39 and App VII [25]

Mostly deposited with other family and
estate papers in Cumbria RO, Kendal at
various dates since 1962.

About 1100 of the numbered items (mainly
newsletters, Nos 827 seq passim) were sold
with other papers at Sotheby's 6 Apr 1925
lots 244-74, 22 May 1933 lots 205-12, and
Christie's 26 Feb 1969 lots 296-309, or by
private sale. Most were acquired by the
Bodleian Library, Oxford (MSS. Don.c.37-40;

Eng.hist.c.306; Eng.lett.c.12, c.196y;
Autogr.c.8; Eng.misc.b.44).

Ten numbered items of Lancashire interest
were acquired before 1955 by Lancaster
Central Library (MSS 6568-77). The deeds of
the Norris family of Speke Hall (pp1-5) were
bought by the Sydney Jones Library,
Liverpool University from JH Le Fleming
in 1930 [NRA 18448].

Some other family papers are among those
of the Pocklington-Senhouse family of
Netherhall deposited in Cumbria RO,
Carlisle [NRA 23769].

LEFROY, TEP Esq
Hillcote, Bournemouth, Hants. 1870
First R, ix and App 56 [1]

The letters and newsletters noticed by the
Report were sold with other papers of
Sir Richard Bulstrode at Sotheby's
3 May 1889 lots 1-79, 216-74. Many then
passed via the Hodgkin collection to the
British Museum (Egerton MSS 3678-84F) or
via the Morrison collection to the
Carl H Pforzheimer Library, New York
(MS 103c, partially catalogued by
AW Thibaudeau, *Bulstrode Papers*, I, 1897),
the National Library of Wales (MS 5389),
the Bodleian Library, Oxford
(MSS. Eng.hist.d.154; Eng.lett.d.72), the
University of Chicago Library (*National
union catalog* MS 64-94) and to private
collectors such as A de Coppet (Sotheby's
4 July 1955 lot 806).

Other papers remain in family possession
[NRA 0918, 8549].

LEGH, WJ Esq, 1st Baron Newton
Lyme Hall, Cheshire. 1872
Third R, xvii and App 268-71 [2]

The papal bull 1437 (p268b) was presented
to Magdalen College, Oxford in 1879
(Eighth R, App I, p269a). The remainder
have been deposited in the John Rylands
Library, Manchester University at various
dates since 1960.

Other family and Newton le Willows
estate papers were deposited in Merseyside
County Archives in 1978.

LEICESTER, Corporation of
1881
Eighth R, xvi-xvii and App I 403-41 [7]

Deposited in Leicestershire RO at various
dates since 1932. *Records of the corporation of
Leicester*, 1956. Additional typescript list
[NRA 6183].

LEICESTER, Earl of
Holkham Hall, Norfolk. 1884, 1907
Ninth R, xvi-xvii, xx and App II 340-75 [8];
Seventeenth R, 126-29; Various collections
IV 313-25 [55]

188 of the 771 MSS in the collection have
been sold since 1927 or accepted for the
Nation in lieu of tax. Most of these have been
acquired by the British Library (Nos 212, 228,
246, 458: Add MSS 47677, 47680, 49365-66)
and the Bodleian Library, Oxford (Nos 166,
245, 460, 468, 663, 672-73, 675, 705, 707,
718: MSS. Holkham misc. 7, 22, 25, 29, 31,
40-41, 43-44, 46). The Leonardo da Vinci MS
(No 699) was sold at Christie's 12 Dec 1980
to A Hammer.

The charters and papers noticed in
Various collections IV remain at Holkham,
apart from the Flitcham charters (pp316-17
which passed with the purchase of the
property to King George V in 1910 and are
now deposited in Norfolk RO [NRA 4636].
Most of the Weasenham charters (p319)
have also been sold. [NRA 12332: photocopy
of the MS catalogue and indexes of Holkham
estate papers].

Other estate papers have been deposited by
solicitors in Norfolk RO [NRA 9306] or
bought by Suffolk RO, Ipswich in 1967
[NRA 16935].

Microfilms of some Holkham MSS and
estate papers are held by the Bodleian Library
and by the Library of Congress, Washington
(*Checklist* E679-F71). Photographic copies of
the early maps and plans (Various collections
IV pp321, 324-25) were deposited in the
British Museum Map Room in 1954.

S De Ricci, *Handlist of MSS in the library
of the Earl of Leicester at Holkham Hall*
(supplement to Bibliographical Society
Transactions No 7), 1932. Microfilm copies of
MS 770, an eight volume catalogue of the
MSS have been placed in the Bodleian
Library, the Library of Congress and,
covering MSS 513-773 only, in the British
Library (M/721).

LEIGH, Lord
Stoneleigh Abbey, Warwicks. 1871
First R, xi; Second R, xiii and App 49 [1]

The Stoneleigh Abbey register and the
'volume of historical and local MSS' were
deposited with other family and estate papers
in the Shakespeare Birthplace Trust RO,
Stratford upon Avon between 1942 and 1958
[Partial lists NRA 4523, 21856].

LEIGHTON, Sir Baldwin Bt
Loton Park, Salop. 1871
Second R, xi and App 64-65 [1]

Remain at Loton Park. Access through
Shropshire RO which also holds a number of

19th cent estate papers deposited by solicitors in 1964.

LEIGHTON, Stanley Esq
Sweeney Hall, Oswestry, Salop. 1885
Tenth R, 18 and App IV 374-78 [13]

Mostly deposited in the National Library of Wales in 1932 as the Mytton of Lloyd and Charlton MSS. *MSS and documents deposited by Major BE Parker-Leighton MP, Sweeney Hall, Oswestry*, typescript, nd. The two MS books entitled 'Remarkable occurrences in Shrewsbury and Salop' and 'Chronicon Salopiense' (pp375-77) are among other records of the Leighton and Parker families sold to, or deposited in, Shropshire RO at various dates since 1948 [NRA 11563].

LEINSTER, Duke of
Carton, Maynooth, co Kildare. 1884
Ninth R, xix and App II 263-93 [8]

The Red Book of the Earls of Kildare remains in family possession. The National Library of Ireland holds a microfilm (n617, p940).

Some Fitzgerald family papers were deposited in the Public Record Office of Northern Ireland in 1975 and others bought by the National Library of Ireland (MSS 18993-99, 20623-25; D 26720).

LENIHAN, Maurice Esq
Limerick. 1870
First R, App 131 [1]

Dispersed by sale. The entry-book of Thomas Arthur MD and the Killaloe consistory court records were among the items acquired by the British Museum in 1881 (Add MSS 31872-88). The Revd J White's collections for the history of Limerick are now in the Royal Irish Academy, Dublin (MS 24.D.21).

LE STRANGE, Hamon Styleman Esq
Hunstanton Hall, Norfolk. 1872-88
Third R, xvii and App 271-74 [2];
Eleventh R, 23-24 and App VII 93-118 [22]

Deposited with Norfolk Record Society in 1952 and now in Norfolk RO.

LEYBORNE POPHAM, FW Esq
Littlecote, Wilts. 1899, 1904
Sixteenth R, 79-86; Leyborne Popham [51]

About a third of the correspondence noticed was sold with other Popham and Clarke family papers to Worcester College, Oxford in 1947 (MSS 266 F.v.1, 267 F.v.2-3; typescript inventory) where it joined the

main group of Clarke papers acquired by the College in 1736.

Other Popham, Clarke and Torrington family papers were sold to the British Museum in 1884 (Egerton MSS 2618-21) and to Trinity College, Dublin before 1810 (MS 749/1-13. NRA 20080).

The official papers of Sir John Popham were presented to the Public Record Office in 1929 (PRO 30/34. NRA 23455). Most of the Civil War papers sold at Sotheby's 5 May 1930 lot 129 have not been traced.

Other family and estate papers have been given or sold to Somerset RO [NRA 1400, 8999], Surrey RO, and Wiltshire RO at various dates since 1929.

LICHFIELD, Dean and Chapter of
1895, 1896
Fourteenth R, 45-46 and App VIII 205-36 [37]

Deposited in Lichfield Joint RO in 1973 apart from the Magnum Registrum Album which remains in the cathedral library (MS Lich 28. NRA 19287).

LIMERICK, Black Book of
1872
Third R, xxvi and App 434-35 [2]

Remains at St Patrick's College, Maynooth. A 19th cent transcript is in Trinity College, Dublin (MS 559 (K.6.14)). The National Library of Ireland has a photographic copy (MS 2704).

LIMERICK, Corporation of
1870
First R, App 131 [1]

The two charters of Cromwell and Charles II are now kept in the Limerick Museum.

See also: Lenihan

LINCOLN, Bishop's Registry
1891
Twelfth R, App IX 573-79 [27]

Deposited in Lincolnshire AO. K Major, *Handlist of the records of the bishop of Lincoln and of the archdeacons of Lincoln and Stow*, 1953, with a typescript supplement of added 19th-20th cent papers [NRA 11190].

LINCOLN, Dean and Chapter of
1890, 1891
Twelfth R, 45 and App IX 553-72 [27]

Deposited in Lincolnshire AO with other capitular records in 1969 [Partial list NRA 5603]. The MSS described by RM Woolley, *Catalogue of the MSS of Lincoln cathedral chapter library*, Oxford, 1927, remain in the chapter library.

LINCOLN, Corporation of
1895, 1896
Fourteenth R, 39-41 and App VIII 1-120 [37]

Deposited in Lincolnshire AO in 1955 except
the royal charters which remain at the
Guildhall [NRA 5742]. W de Gray Birch,
*Catalogue of the royal charters and other
documents and list of books . . .* , 1906.
Lincolnshire Archives Committee,
Archivists' reports, 1948-50 pp19-20,
1950-51 pp9-15, *1955-56* pp13-15.

LINCOLN, District Probate Registry
1891
Twelfth R, App IX 573 [27]

Deposited in Lincolnshire AO, 1955.

LINDSEY, Earl of
Uffington House, Lincs. 1895-1946
Fourteenth R, 28-29 and App IX 367-457 [38];
Twenty-Second R, 11; Lindsey [79]

The Osborne correspondence 1667-96
(Fourteenth R) has not been seen since 1931,
when the 12th Earl (d 1938) removed some of
it from the Public Record Office, to which he
had taken it for repair after 'recent damage
by water'.
    The rest of the papers noticed were
deposited by his daughter Lady Muriel
Barclay-Harvey in the Bodleian Library,
Oxford (Dep.c.149-51) in 1955 except the
deeds bought from the Dering collection
(p vi) which were placed in Kent AO.

**LIVINGSTONE, Thomas Livingstone
Fenton Esq**
Westquarter, Stirlingshire. 1879
Seventh R, xvi and App 732-35 [6]

The twenty-one charters and other family
documents described have not been traced.

LLAN STEPHAN see Williams, Sir John Bt

LLANWRIN see Evans

LLOYD, S Zachary Esq
Areley Hall, Worcs. 1885
Tenth R, 20 and App IV 444-50 [13]

Mostly deposited with other family papers in
Birmingham Reference Library, 1939
[NRA 23593].

LODER SYMONDS, Captain FC
Hinton Waldrist Manor, Berks. 1892
Thirteenth R, 47-48 and App IV 378-404 [31]

Most were sold privately to Lord Brotherton
c1933 with other family and estate papers

through JA Symington, a Leeds book dealer
and librarian, and subsequently passed to the
Brotherton Library, Leeds University in 1935.
    Some petitions (pp395-96) are among the
papers of JA Symington acquired by Leeds
Archives Department at various dates since
1962. Colonel Henry Marten's draft pamphlets
(pp400-01) were sold separately to
Lord Fairfax of Cameron c1933. John Donne's
letter and Sir Henry Marten's notes
(pp383-84) were sold to the Houghton
Library, Harvard University (fMS Eng 930)
in 1942.
    Further papers from Hinton Waldrist
deposited in Berkshire RO in 1952 and 1958
include Robert Loder's farm accounts
(pp381-82) and an almanack 1655 of
Colonel Henry Marten [NRA 0721]. An
album of miscellaneous family papers
remains in family possession.

LONDON, Bishop of
1914, 1917
Eighteenth R, 201-04; Various collections
VII 1-9 [55]

Mostly deposited in the Guildhall Library,
London at various dates since 1956. The
Colonial papers (pp8-9) have been placed in
Lambeth Palace Library where the American
section has been calendared by WW Manross,
Fulham Palace papers, Oxford, 1965.

LONDON, Dean and Chapter of St Paul's
1883
Ninth R, viii and App I 1-72 [8]

Deposited in the Guildhall Library, London,
1980.

LONDON, Catholic Chapter of
1876
Fifth R, App 463-70 [4]

Given to the Archbishop of Westminster in
1879 and kept at Brompton Oratory where
they were rearranged and merged with other
series of papers before transfer to the
Diocesan Archives, Archbishop's House,
Westminster in 1907.
    The volume of Douai College visitations
1612-26 (p463) was subsequently transferred
to St Edmunds College, Ware.
    Some other records of the Old Brotherhood
brought together at Oscott College,
Birmingham were transferred to the
Diocesan Archives, Westminster in 1968,
see *Catalogue of part of the archives of the
Old Brotherhood of the English Secular Clergy*,
Catholic Record Society, 1968.

LONDON see also British Museum
(Welsh MSS); House of Lords; Inner
Temple; Lambeth Palace; Queen Anne's

Bounty; Royal College of Physicians; Royal Institution; Southwark; Trinity House; Westminster; Williams, Dr, Library of

LONGLEAT see Bath

LONSDALE, Earl of
Lowther Castle, Westmorland and Whitehaven Castle, Cumberland. 1892, 1893
Thirteenth R, 32-35 and App VII [33]

Deposited with other family papers in Cumbria RO, Carlisle at various dates between 1963 and 1975 [NRA 17777], apart from some of the documents at Whitehaven (including the letter of William Penn) which have been missing since 1914.

Seven miscellaneous MSS from the library at Lowther Castle not noticed by the Report were sold at Sotheby's, 12 July 1937.

LOSELEY see More Molyneux

LOSTWITHIEL, Corporation of
1901
Sixteenth R, 101-02; Various collections I 327-37 [55]

Deposited in Cornwall RO, 1968-71.

LOTHIAN, Marquess of
Blickling Hall, Norfolk. 1870-1907
First R, x and App 14 [1]; Seventeenth R, 45-51; Lothian [62]

Most of the items noticed were deposited with Norfolk Record Society in 1941 and are now in Norfolk RO with other family papers [NRA 4641]. The folio psalter and the volume of Anglo-Saxon homilies (First R, p14) were sold with other MSS in 1932 and are in the Pierpont Morgan Library, New York (M 776) and Princeton University Library (Scheide collection MS 66) respectively. Some further MS books (First R, p14) remain at Blickling Hall with the William Ivory plans (Lothian, p441) and other papers relating to the Hall which is now the property of the National Trust.

LOTHIAN, Marquess of
Newbattle, Midlothian. 1870
First R, xii and App 116-17 [1]

The fifteen volumes of papers listed are among the Kerr family papers deposited in the Scottish Record Office at various dates since 1932 (GD 40).

112 volumes of MSS and papers were also presented to the National Library of Scotland in 1950 (MSS 5730-5841).

LOWNDES, George Alan Esq
Barrington Hall, Essex. 1876, 1879
Fifth R, xi [4]; Seventh R, xiv and App 537-89 [6]

Most of the papers and early deeds were sold to the British Museum in 1886 with some other Barrington family correspondence (Egerton MSS 2643-51; Add Ch 28313-637).

The remaining papers including Sir Thomas Barrington's parliamentary diaries 1621 (p538), the Hatfield Priory grant c1190 (p579), the fragment of the Hatfield Broad Oak cartulary (p581), the 14th cent extent (p587) and the Providence Island and Bermuda papers (p589) were moved to the library of Hatfield Broad Oak Church in 1908 and have subsequently been acquired by Essex RO with other strays from the archive at various dates since 1939 [NRA 6600].

LUCAS, Baroness see Cowper, Countess

LUTTRELL, GF Esq
Dunster Castle, Somerset. 1870-87
First R, x and App 56-57 [1]; Tenth R, 23 and App VI 72-81 [15]

Deposited with other family and estate papers in Somerset RO, 1958 [NRA 6670].

LYDD, Corporation of
1876
Fifth R, xvii and App 516-33 [4]

Remain at Lydd Town Hall in the custody of the town clerk [NRA 8784].

LYONS, Dr RD
Merrion Square, Dublin. 1870, 1871
First R, xiii; Second R, xxi and App 231-57 [1]

Bought from PE O'Donnell by Trinity College, Dublin in 1919 [NRA 20078].

LYTTELTON, Lord
Hagley Hall, Worcs. 1871
Second R, xi and App 36-39 [1]

The bound volumes of letter books and family correspondence (pp36-37) remain at Hagley Hall, apart from some papers of the 1st Lord Lyttelton as Governor of South Carolina (p36) sold privately in 1953 to the William L Clements Library, University of Michigan and some others of his as Governor of Jamaica sold at Sotheby's 8 Apr 1963 lots 510, 511 to the William R Perkins Library, Duke University, Durham, North Carolina.

Most of the correspondence and deeds noticed on pp37-39 were auctioned at

Sotheby's 12 Dec 1978. A large number of Halesowen Abbey court rolls and other Hagley Hall deeds were sold privately in the same year to Birmingham Reference Library where they had been deposited on loan since 1931 [NRA 24190].

Further family and estate papers have been deposited at various dates since 1964 in Hereford and Worcester RO, Worcester, some by solicitors [NRA 12165, 14331, 14545]. A few papers were also sold privately to the Record Office in 1978.

LYTTELTON ANNESLEY, Lt-General
1893
Thirteenth R, App VI 261-78 [32]

The diary of the 1st Earl of Anglesey for the years 1671-75 was presented to the British Museum in 1923 (Add MS 40860; cf Add MS 18730).

MACARTNEY, Earl, Governor of Madras
Hugh Hyndman LL D, Belfast. 1884
Ninth R, xx and App II 330-40 [8]

The five volumes of Indian papers noticed were presented to the Public Record Office of Northern Ireland by Colonel JVO Macartney Filgate in 1961 with other family papers (D 2225/4/55-59. NRA 6465).

The 1st Earl's papers have otherwise become widely scattered. The two largest collections are now in the British Library and the Bodleian Library, Oxford.

MACAULAY, the late Colonel
HG Bennett, Sparkford, Somerset. 1874
Fourth R, xv-xvi and App 397-404 [3]

The papers of John Wilkes which the Report describes were sold to the British Museum in 1878 (Add MSS 30865-96).

MACCLESFIELD, Earl of
Shirburn Castle, Oxon. 1870
First R, ix and App 34-41 [1]

The official and private papers and correspondence of John Ellis (1643 ?-1738), Under Secretary of State 1695-1705, of which the Report notices only three small parts, were bought by the British Museum in 1872 (Add MSS 28875-956). The letters of Matthew Prior (p ix) are in Add MS 28928. Those of George Stepney and James Cresset (pp34-41) are distributed throughout the collection.

Other MSS at Shirburn Castle, but not open for research, include a chronicle of Hyde Abbey (ed E Edwards, *Liber monasterii de Hyda*, Rolls ser, 1866), a small group of mathematical papers and letters of Sir Isaac Newton, and two volumes of other scientific letters and papers 1616-1742. Most

of the letters were printed by SP Rigaud, *Correspondence of scientific men of the seventeenth century*, 2 vols, 1841-62.

Transcripts of some of the estate papers were given to the Bodleian Library, Oxford in 1966 [NRA 0904]. Some Staffordshire manorial documents were deposited in Staffordshire RO in 1973 [NRA 17371].

McDOUALL, Colonel James
Logan, Wigtownshire. 1874
Fourth R, xxiii and App 535-36 [3]

Deposited in the Scottish Record Office, 1943 (GD 141).

Some other family papers 17th-20th cent are in private possession [NRA 23862].

MACKESON, HB Esq
Hythe, Kent. 1871
Second R, xi-xii and App 91-92 [1]

The miscellaneous and fragmentary papers listed are thought to have been restored by Mr HB Mackeson (d 1894) to their proper places in the Hythe Borough records as these were identified. They are not otherwise traceable.

Some other Mackeson family papers were deposited in Kent AO in 1955 [NRA 5978].

MACRAY, Revd William Dunn
Ducklington Rectory, Oxon. 1892
Thirteenth R, App IV 507-08 [31]

The five miscellaneous volumes listed by the Report were sold through Blackwell's of Oxford between 1892 and 1916. No 4 was subsequently presented to the National Library of Scotland in 1945 (MS 3545). The others have not been traced. For No 2 see *Bibliothèque de l'Ecole des Chartes*, liii, 1892, pp684-85.

MAINWARING, Sir Philip T Bt
Peover Hall, Cheshire. 1885
Tenth R, 4 and App IV 199-210 [13]

Mostly deposited with other family papers in the John Rylands Library, Manchester University in 1921 and 1955. *Handlist of the Mainwaring and Jodrell MSS*, Manchester, 1923. [NRA 4799]. Subsequently purchased by the Library in 1973 apart from seventy-five items which were removed, some for sale at Sotheby's 20 Nov 1973 lots 18-194 passim.

At the latter sale the Bodleian Library, Oxford bought many papers of Roger Whitley MP [NRA 23480] and Sir Thomas Mainwaring's Legitimacy of Amicia (MS. Top.Cheshire c.19). Cheshire RO bought the two volumes of Sir Thomas Mainwaring's diary 1648-58, 1674-88. The Osborn Collection, Beinecke Library,

Yale University bought the letters from
Sir Joseph Williamson to Roger Whitley
1673-74.

A few MSS remain in family possession.

MAJENDIE, Lewis Esq
Hedingham Castle, Essex. 1876
Fifth R, ix and App 321-23 [4]

Remain at Hedingham Castle, except for the
mortuary roll (pp321-22) which was sold to the
British Museum in 1903 (Egerton MS 2849).
Not open for research. A few manorial
documents not listed by the Report and a
microfilm of the extent of the honour of
Hedingham 1592 (p322) have been placed in
Essex RO. *Guide to the Essex RO*, 1969,
pp122-24.

MALET, Sir Alexander Bt
Queensberry Place, Kensington, London.
1876, 1879
Fifth R, vii-ix and App 308-21 [4];
Seventh R, xiii-xiv and App 428-33 [6]

Mostly sold to the British Museum in 1882
(Add MSS 32091-96). A few of the
unbound papers (Fifth R, p321. NRA 18542)
were sold by King and Chasemore's,
Pulborough, 14 June 1977 lots 845-50 when
the Newton Toney estate papers were bought
by Wiltshire RO.

MANCHESTER, Chetham's Library
1871
Second R, xii and App 156-58 [1]

The volume of 16th and 17th cent historical
collections relating to Ireland remains in the
library as MS Mun A. 6(4) 77.

Other MSS there are described in *Bibliotheca
Chethamensis*, 6 vols, Manchester, 1791-1883,
of which NRA 17002 is a typescript summary
and supplement. See also *Bulletin of the
Institute of Historical Research*, x, 1932-33,
pp69-72.

MANCHESTER, Duke of
Kimbolton Castle, Hunts. 1870, 1881
First R, x and App 12-13 [1]; Eighth R,
App II [7]

The Rous Roll was sold to the British Museum
in 1955 (Add MS 48976).

Most of the other papers noticed were
deposited in the Public Record Office from
1880 until 1969. Nos 1-114 were then
presented to the John Rylands Library,
Manchester University. Nos 682-98, 718-902
were returned into family possession. The
remainder were sold at Sotheby's 23 Mar 1970
lots 389-421 (miscellaneous single
documents), 5 May 1970 at Sotheby Parke
Bernet New York (Virginia papers),
22 June 1970 lots 267-68 (John Donne MSS),

20 July 1970 lots 606-10 (papers of the
4th Duke of Manchester as ambassador to
France 1783-84), 26 Oct 1970 lots 336-67
(papers of the 1st and 2nd Earls of
Manchester, Sir Nathaniel Rich, the 4th Duke
of Manchester etc).

Eventual recipients of substantial groups
of the papers sold include the National
Library of Ireland (Nos 172-202a.
British Library microfilm RP 536), the
Arents Collection for the History of Tobacco,
New York Public Library, and Bermuda
Archives (Nos 203-426. British Library
microfilm RP 420), RM Willcocks (121 items
from Nos 427-669 passim, of which the
House of Lords Record Office has
photocopies), Cambridgeshire RO,
Huntingdon (Nos 671-81) and the
William L Clements Library, University of
Michigan (Nos 946-1287. British Library
microfilm RP 517).

Other family and estate papers from
Kimbolton Castle were deposited in
Cambridgeshire RO, Huntingdon in 1948
and 1954 [NRA 0902]. These included seven
literary MSS subsequently withdrawn for
sale at Sotheby's 23 June 1975 lots 266-67.

MANNING, Cardinal see Westminster,
Catholic Archbishop of

MANNING, Revd CR
Diss, Norfolk. 1885
Tenth R, 26 and App IV 458-63 [13]

Most of the documents listed were sold to the
British Museum in 1891 and 1894
(Add MSS 33985-90, 34560-64;
Add Ch 37399-459). Those of 'purely local
interest' (p458) are now in Norfolk RO
[NRA 4646]. A few items remain untraced.

Some further MSS not listed by the
Report were sold at Sotheby's 20 July 1899
with Canon Manning's library. From these a
psalter is now British Library Add MS 38822.

MANVERS, Earl
Thoresby Park, Notts. 1884
Ninth R, xvi and App II 375-79 [8]

Sold in 1942 to the British Museum
(Egerton MSS 3516-3660; Egerton
Ch 2301-8836) apart from the
Buckinghamshire deeds and charters which
were sold to the Bodleian Library, Oxford
(MSS. Top.Notts.c.2; Maps c.5,19(1)).

Other estate papers were subsequently
placed in Nottingham University Library
[NRA 3707].

MAR AND KELLIE, Earl of
Alloa House, Clackmannanshire. 1904-38
Seventeenth R, 130-38; Twenty-First R, 12;
Mar and Kellie; Supplementary Report [60]

Presented with other family papers to the
Scottish Record Office, 1957 (GD 124).
Typescript inventory.

MARCHMONT see Hume Campbell

MARLBOROUGH, Duke of
Blenheim, Oxon. 1881
Eighth R, x-xi and App I 1-60 [7]

Ten of the St Albans Abbey charters,
forty-two autograph letters and some American
letters and papers of Charles Spencer,
3rd Earl of Sunderland were sold at
Sotheby's 1 July 1920 lots 7-251. Of these, a
number relating to civil disturbances in
New York and Maryland were bought by the
Huntington Library, San Marino in 1926
(*National union catalog* MS 61-1556) and by
the Maryland Historical Society (MS 737).

The remainder of the archive was accepted
for the Nation in lieu of tax in 1977 and
allocated to the British Library
(Add MSS 61101-710).

The papers belonging to the Blenheim
settled estate remain at Blenheim Estate Office
but are not open for research [NRA 8130].

MARSH, T Chisenhale Esq
Gaynes Park, Theydon Garnon, Essex. 1872
Third R, xvii and App 274 [2]

Presented to Essex RO, 1959. Other family
and estate papers were deposited there in
1968 [NRA 21911].

MARYON WILSON, Sir John Bt
Charlton Estate Office, London. 1876
Fifth R, viii and App 304-05 [4]

The Icelandic Jónsbók (p304) was sold in 1931
and is now Princeton University Library
MS 62. The two volumes of family
correspondence (p305) and some other
correspondence and papers were presented
to the British Museum by Viscountess Gough
in 1958 (Add MSS 49605-08). Further groups
of family and estate papers have been
deposited in Greater London RO
[NRA 10894 and unlisted] and Essex RO
[NRA 7849].

MAXWELL STUART see Stuart,
Hon Henry Constable Maxwell

MEADLEY, Cornelius Esq
1870
First R, App 110 [1]

The single volume noticed, a precedent book
'of no historical or legal value', has not been
traced.

MENDLESHAM, Parish of
1876
Fifth R, xviii and App 593-96 [4]

Deposited in Suffolk RO, Ipswich in 1963
apart from the two inspeximuses of James I
(p595: Nos 25, 26) retained by the incumbent,
and Henry Jesop's will (p596) which cannot
now be traced. [NRA Suffolk parish reports].

MENZIES, Sir Robert Bt
Castle Menzies, Perthshire. 1877
Sixth R, xviii and App 688-709 [5]

Dispersed with other papers from Castle
Menzies after the death of Sir Neil
Menzies Bt in 1910.

Eventual recipients include the
Scottish Record Office (GD 50/128:
Nos 75-77, 83-84, 87-88, 90-92, 98-99, 102,
127, 130, 132-34, 170, 176; GD 1/408/1:
No 9), the National Library of Scotland
(MS 3741/1: Nos 138-52) and the
West Highlands Museum, Fort William
(Nos 36, 45, 72, 74).

Further family papers have been acquired
by the Scottish Record Office and by the
National Library of Scotland [NRA 20934].

MERTHYR TYDFIL see Reynolds

MERTTENS, F Esq
Rothley Temple, Leics and Bilton Rise,
Warwicks. 1914, 1919
Eighteenth R, 230; Various collections
VII 376-88 [55]

Deposited with other legal and estate papers
in Leicester Museum before 1928 and
subsequently transferred to Leicestershire RO.

MIDDLETON, Lord
Wollaton Hall, Notts. 1911, 1919
Eighteenth R, 14-21; Middleton [69]

Mostly deposited in Nottingham University
Library at various dates since 1947 with other
family and estate papers [NRA 7428].
Microfilm copies are in the Library of
Congress, Washington (*Checklist* F 73-207).

Glanville's De Proprietatibus Rerum (p240)
was sold with three other MSS at
Christie's 15 June 1925 and is now in
Columbia University Libraries, New York
(Plimpton MS 263).

Some of the MSS relating to Kent were
given to Sevenoaks Public Library in 1930

and transferred to Kent AO in 1963 [NRA 18189]. The fragments of the 8th cent vulgate (pp196, 611) and the Oswald Cartulary (pp196-99) were bought for the British Museum in 1937 and 1946 (Add MSS 45025, 46204).

The missing second volume of Cassandra Willoughby's account of the family was found in 1956 and presented to Nottingham University Library by an anonymous donor.

MIDLETON, Viscount
1870
First R, ix and App 44 [1]

The nine volumes of correspondence and papers noticed were deposited in the Guildford Muniment Room, Surrey RO in 1976, to join other groups of family correspondence and estate papers placed there at various dates since 1953 [NRA 1351].

Another group of correspondence and papers mainly of the Hon Charles Brodrick, Archbishop of Cashel 1801-22, was sold to the National Library of Ireland in 1954 (MSS 8861-99, 9410-23).

MILDMAY, Sir Henry Bt
Dogmersfield Park, Hants. 1876
Fifth R, viii and App 307 [4]

Abraham Tucker's Light of Nature was presented to the Bodleian Library, Oxford in 1939 (MS. Eng.misc.c.261-64). Some further MSS not reported on were sold at Sotheby's 18 Apr 1907 with the library from Dogmersfield, from which Sir Henry Mildmay's official copy of the minute book of a sub-committee of the Parliamentary Commission for Essex 1643-54 is now British Library Add MS 37491.

A large number of other family papers have been deposited in Hampshire RO at various dates since 1950 [NRA 5382].

MILDMAY, Captain Hervey G St John
Hazelgrove House, Queen Camel, Somerset. 1879
Seventh R, xiv and App 590-96 [6]

Deposited in Somerset RO with other family papers in 1949 [NRA 21219]. The papers relating to the Mildmay family of Marks were subsequently transferred to Essex RO in 1955 [NRA 5383] where those of the Mildmay family of Moulsham Hall have also been deposited at various dates since 1940 [NRA 10733].

MILNE HOME, Colonel David
Wedderburn Castle, Berwickshire. 1902, 1904
Sixteenth R, 122; Milne Home [57]

Deposited in the Scottish Record Office, 1971, 1978 (GD 267. NRA 11620).

MOLONY, Revd Michael
Kilbride, co Wicklow. 1872
Third R, xxvi and App 432-34 [2]

The single item noticed, Dr Hugh Howard's Parliamentary history of Ireland, is now in the Gilbert collection, Dublin Public Libraries (MSS 88-89).

MONBODDO see Burnett family

MONEY KYRLE, Major
Homme House, Much Marcle, Herefs. 1907
Seventeenth R, 120-21; Various collections IV 96-139 [55]

Remain in family possession. Other family correspondence and papers not described by the Report have been deposited by Mrs Elizabeth Shetliffe in Hereford and Worcester RO, Hereford at various dates since 1971.

MONTAGU OF BEAULIEU, Lord
Palace House, Beaulieu, Hants. 1900, 1904
Sixteenth R, 59-62; Montagu [53]

Remain at Palace House [NRA 4880]. Some of the aviation correspondence and papers of the 2nd Baron were deposited in the Liddell Hart Centre, King's College, London in 1965 and 1973 [NRA 11393].

MONTROSE, Royal Burgh of
1871
Second R, xx and App 205-06 [1]

At Montrose Town House in the custody of the director of administration, County Buildings, Forfar [NRA 10426].

MONTROSE, Duke of
Buchanan Castle, Stirlingshire. 1871, 1872
Second R, xvi and App 165-77 [1]; Third R, xxi-xxii and App 368-402 [2]

Deposited with other family papers in the Scottish Record Office, 1966 (GD 220). Typescript inventory.

MORAY, Earl of
Donibristle, Fife. 1877
Sixth R, xvii and App 634-73 [5]

In family possession at Darnaway Castle [NRA 10983].

MORAY, Charles Home Drummond Esq
Abercairny, Blair Drummond and Ardoch,
Perthshire. 1872, 1885
Third R, xxiii–xxiv and App 416-20 [2];
Tenth R, 37-42 and App I 81-199 [10]

Presented or loaned to the Scottish Record
Office with other family muniments at
various dates since 1939 (GD 24).
Gifts and Deposits i, pp44-52. Typescript
inventory.

MORE, R Jasper Esq
Shipton and Linley Halls, Salop. 1885
Tenth R, 19 and App IV 407-08 [13]

The illuminated letters of credence of James I
and the medieval bestiary were sold before
1947. The Shipton parish registers 1538-1792
and Wenlock Priory roll of fines have been
deposited with other More and Mytton
family papers in Shropshire RO [NRA 11563].
Other items noticed remain at Linley.

MORE MOLYNEUX, William Esq
Loseley Park, Surrey. 1879
Seventh R, xiv–xv and App 596-681 [6];
Seventeenth R, 12

Several hundred documents including many
noticed by the Reports were sold between
1910 and 1940. Of these, 712 items including
most of Sir Thomas Cawarden's papers and
the letters of John Donne are now in the
Folger Library, Washington [NRA 8125;
British Library microfilm M/437]. Fourteen
bound volumes of correspondence remain at
Loseley (access through the Guildford
Muniment Room, Surrey RO). The
remainder have been placed in the Guildford
Muniment Room with other family and
estate papers [NRA 9475].

MORPETH, Corporation of
1877
Sixth R, App 526-38 [5]

Deposited in Northumberland RO, 1962
[NRA 7874].

MORRISON, Alfred Esq
Fonthill House, Wilts and Carlton House
Terrace, London. 1884
Ninth R, xvii–xviii and App II 406-93 [8]

Dispersed with the rest of the Morrison
collection in sales at Sotheby's 10 Dec 1917
lots 1-771, 15 Apr 1918 lots 772-1769,
9 Dec 1918 lots 1770-2672 and 5 May 1919
lots 2673-3313.
    Most of the bound volumes (pp407-10)
and some of the unbound letters (18 lots)
were bought by the Carl H Pforzheimer
Library, New York. Eventual recipients of
other items traced include the British Library

(Add MSS 39672-73, 39757, 39779-93,
39839-42, 40663, 41132, 41178F, 41340I,
42176, 44936, 45680C), the National Library
of Scotland (MS 3420: Godolphin family
correspondence, p455), Lambeth Palace
Library (MS 1834: letters from
Henry Compton, Bishop of London, p460),
the Duke of Rutland (miscellaneous autograph
letters bequeathed by Captain CL Lindsay),
and various American libraries.

MORTON, Earl of
Dalmahoy, Midlothian. 1871
Second R, xviii and App 183-85 [1]

The twelve volumes of papers and
correspondence noticed by the Report were
sold to the National Library of Scotland
in 1927 (MSS 73-84).
    Other family papers were deposited in the
Scottish Record Office in 1936 (GD 150).
Typescript inventory.

MOSTYN, Lord
Mostyn Hall, nr Holywell, Flints. 1870-1904
First R, x and App 44-45 [1]; Fourth R,
App 347-63 [3]; Fifteenth R, 49;
Sixteenth R, 132; Welsh MSS I i [48]

Most of the Welsh MSS were sold privately to
the National Library of Wales in 1918
(MSS 3021-76; *Handlist*, I, 1943, pp261-63).
The other MSS noticed were mostly sold at
Sotheby's 13 July 1920 and at Christie's
24 Oct 1974.
    Immediate or eventual recipients of MSS
sold in 1920 include the Bodleian Library,
the British Library (Add MSS 40000, 57533;
Egerton MSS 3029, 3049; Yates Thompson
MS 47), Cardiff Central Library, London
University Library and the National Library
of Wales (MSS 3020E, 16966B).
Thirty-one MSS have been traced to
American collections.
    From the sale in 1974 eighteen MSS were
bought by the National Library of Wales
(MSS 21238B-47B, 21693) and others by
Lambeth Palace Library, Westminster Abbey
Library, and Wiltshire, Cheshire and
Hampshire ROs.
    The family papers deposited in the
University College of North Wales, Bangor
[NRA 22953] include Nos 96, 232-36, 239-54
and the newsletters (First R, pp44-45).
Other family papers have been deposited in
Clwyd RO, Hawarden at various dates since
1960 [NRA 17858]. Some further family
papers remain at Mostyn.

MOUNT EDGCUMBE, Earl of
Mount Edgcumbe, Cornwall. 1871
Second R, x and App 20-24 [1]

The papers listed by the Report were all
destroyed by enemy action in 1941. Other

family and estate papers have been deposited in Cornwall RO at various dates since 1954 [NRA 4207].

MUNCASTER, Lord
Muncaster Castle, Cumberland. 1885
Tenth R, 15-16 and App IV 223-98 [13]

Admiral Sir John Pennington's journal (pp275-96) is now National Maritime Museum MS JOD/1. Most of the other papers noticed are among the Pennington Ramsden family and estate papers deposited in Cumbria RO, Carlisle at various dates since 1963 [Partial list NRA 12093].

Some further family papers have been deposited in the John Rylands Library, Manchester University. *Handlist of Crawford muniments*, 1976, pp83-87. The rest, including papers of the 11th and 12th Dukes of Somerset, remain at Muncaster Castle [NRA 24077].

MURRAY, Sir Patrick Keith Bt
Ochtertyre, Perthshire. 1872
Third R, xxiv and App 408-13 [2]

Deposited in the Scottish Record Office in 1962 and subsequently sold to the National Library of Scotland in 1974 (Acc 6026. NRA 20932).

MYDDLETON BIDDULPH, Colonel Robert
Chirk Castle, Denbighs. 1871
Second R, xi and App 73-74 [1]

Mostly among the family papers deposited in the National Library of Wales, 1931-32 [Partial list NRA 10568]. These however do not include the History of the Kings and Princes of Wales 16th cent, and Queen Elizabeth's instructions to Henry Earl of Pembroke 1586.

NAPIER, Colonel
1870
First R, x and App 57

The Spanish papers noticed by the Report have not been traced.

NEW ROMNEY, Corporation of
1874-77
Fourth R, xviii and App 439-42 [3];
Fifth R, xvii-xviii and App 533-54 [4];
Sixth R, App 540-45 [5]

Deposited in Kent AO at various dates since 1960 apart from a few items retained at New Romney Town Hall [NRA 10066].

NEWARK, Corporation of
1890, 1891
Twelfth R, 47 and App IX 538 [27]

Mostly now kept at the Town Hall or in Newark Museum. The quarter sessions rolls and some charity records are deposited in Nottinghamshire RO. Some other charity records are in the parish church.

NEWBATTLE see Lothian

NORFOLK, Duke of
Norfolk House, London SW. 1903-19
Sixteenth R, 108; Eighteenth R, 225;
Various collections II 337-47, VII 153-246 [55]

Remain in family possession at Arundel Castle. Access through the librarian.
FW Steer, *Arundel Castle archives*, 4 vols, 1968-80, and *Catalogue of the Earl Marshal's papers at Arundel Castle*, Harleian Society cxv, cxvi, 1963-64.

Some Yorkshire, Nottinghamshire and Derbyshire estate papers are in Sheffield Central Library. A few are among the Bagshawe collection presented to it in 1956 [NRA 7871], others were deposited there in 1960 (*Catalogue of the Arundel Castle MSS*, Sheffield, 1965) and in 1970.

See also: Herries; Northampton

NORTHAMPTON, Marquess of
Castle Ashby, Northants. 1872
Third R, xvii and App 209-10 [2]

The genealogical MS noticed by the Report was later presented to the 15th Duke of Norfolk and is now at Arundel Castle.

Most of the family and estate papers remain at Castle Ashby [NRA 21088]. A few were deposited in Devon RO in 1969 [NRA 16369] and in Cornwall RO in 1970 [NRA 5010]. Seventeen literary MSS were sold at Christie's 8 Mar 1978 lots 293-300 and 5 July 1978 lot 47. Thirteen of these were bought by the British Library (Add MSS 60273-85).

NORTHUMBERLAND, Duke of
Alnwick Castle, Northumberland and Syon House, Mddx. 1872-77
Third R, xii and App 45-125 (Alnwick Castle) [2]; Fifth R, xi [4]; Sixth R, xi and App 221-33 (Syon House) [5]

Most of the items noticed are now at Alnwick Castle. The case paper (Sixth R, p232) is at Syon House with other parliamentary and common law proceedings. The manorial records for Isleworth (ibid pp232-33) and East Bedfont with Hatton were deposited in the Greater London RO in 1977. Microfilm copies of the

Northumberland papers made for the Library of Congress, Washington (*Checklist* F 233-950) may be consulted in the British Library (M/280-416) with the prior permission of the Duke of Northumberland.

Some other papers at Alnwick and Syon have also now been listed by the Commission [NRA 0836].

See also: Leconfield

NORWICH, Bishop's Registry
1870
First R, App 86-87 [1]

Deposited in Norfolk RO, 1963 [NRA 9364].

NORWICH, Dean and Chapter of
1870
First R, App 87-89 [1]

Deposited in Norfolk RO, 1975, except Bartholomew de Cotton's Historia Anglicana (p89) retained in the cathedral library.

NORWICH, Corporation of
1870
First R, App 102-04 [1]

Deposited in Norfolk RO, 1962. W Hudson and JC Tingey, *Revised catalogue of the records of the city of Norwich*, 1898 and typescript supplement [NRA 6667].

NOTTINGHAM, Corporation of
1870
First R, App 105-06 [1]

Deposited in Nottinghamshire RO, 1977. WH Stevenson and others, *Records of the borough of Nottingham*, 9 vols, 1882-1956. *Historical records of Nottingham corporation*, leaflet nd [NRA 3015].

O'CONOR, Charles Owen, the O'Conor Don
Clonalis, Castlerea, co Roscommon. 1871, 1884
Second R, xxi and App 223-27 [1]; Eighth R, xviii and App I 441-92 [7]

Remain at Clonalis except the Duanaire Mhéig Shamhradháin (Second R, p223 No 1) bought by the National Library of Ireland in 1971 (MS G 1200). *The O'Conor papers*, ed GW and JE Dunleavy, Madison, 1977.

O'DONNELL, Sir Richard Bt
1874
Fourth R, xxiv and App 584-88 [3]

The psalter of St Columba has been deposited with the Royal Irish Academy, Dublin since 1843.

ONSLOW, Earl of
Clandon Park, Surrey. 1895, 1896
Fourteenth R, 29-31 and App IX 458-524 [38]

The single item noticed, Speaker Arthur Onslow's book of anecdotes 1711, was deposited in the House of Lords Record Office in 1972 with his annotated calendar of the journals 1728-61, Edward Jefferies' book of precedents 1708, the Earl of Nottingham's treatise on impeachments 1678 and the establishment of Queen Caroline's Household 1730.

Most of the family and estate papers have been deposited in the Guildford Muniment Room, Surrey RO at various dates since 1947 [NRA 1088]. Some Essex manorial documents were deposited in Essex RO in 1940 [NRA 21547]. A few grants and letters patent remain at Clandon Park.

ORANMORE AND BROWNE, Lord
Castle MacGarrett, Claremorris, co Mayo. 1910, 1919
Eighteenth R, 135; Various collections VI 438-39 [55]

The single item noticed, the letter from General Monck, remains in family possession.

ORFORD, Corporation of
1907
Seventeenth R, 123-34; Various collections IV 255-78 [55]

Deposited with other borough records in Suffolk RO, Ipswich, 1964 [NRA 19130].

ORLEBAR, Richard Esq
Hinwick House, Beds. 1872
Third R, xix and App 274-76 [2]

The Canons Ashby cartulary (p274) was sold to the British Museum in 1924 (Egerton MS 3033). The parson and churchwardens' dispute (p274), the presentments 1616 (p275b) and the Bedford election papers (p276) are among the family and estate papers deposited in Bedfordshire RO at various dates since 1932 [NRA 0118].

The Sharnbrook manorial survey 1617 (p274), the Orders for the better regulation of the King's Bench (p275) and a MS of Samuel Newton's Synoptis Mathematica were sold at Sotheby's 15 July 1952 lots 291-93, when the survey was bought by Bedfordshire RO. The rest of the material noticed remains in family possession at Hinwick House, bound in three volumes with other papers.

The family's Sussex estate papers were deposited with Sussex Archaeological Society in 1948 [NRA 12248]. Other family papers are included in the Vorley collection bought by Bedfordshire RO in 1968 [NRA 19524].

ORMONDE, Marquess of
Kilkenny Castle. 1871-1926
Second R, xxi and App 209-10 [1]; Third R,
xxv and App 425-30 [2]; Fourth R, xxiv and
App 539-73 [3]; Sixth R, xix and App 719-80 [5];
Seventh R, xvii and App II 737-834 [6];
Eighth R, xviii and App I 499-552 [7];
Ninth R, xix and App II 126-81 [8]; Tenth R,
42 and App V 1-106 [14]; Thirteenth R, 55;
Fourteenth R, 51 and App VII (Ormonde I);
Fifteenth R, 46; Sixteenth R, 122-32;
Seventeenth R, 139-43; Eighteenth R, 257-84;
Nineteenth R, 41-47; Ormonde II;
Ormonde new series I-VIII [36]

Bought by the National Library of Ireland
in 1951 except the letters calendared in
Ormonde I, pp4-89, 105-18 and Ormonde
n.s.IV, pp599-664 which are now in the
British Library (MS Loan 37).

**ORMSBY GORE, JR Esq,
1st Baron Harlech**
Brogyntyn, Oswestry, Salop. 1871, 1874
Second R, xi and App 84-88 [1]; Fourth R,
xv and App 379-97 [3]

Deposited in the National Library of Wales
in 1934 and 1938, with other family and
estate papers. *Clenennau letters and papers*,
ed T Jones Pierce, pt I, 1947.

OSBORN, Sir George Bt
Chicksands Priory, Beds. 1871
Second R, xi and App 65 [1]

The papers relating to Guernsey
16th-17th cent, and to the siege of Castle
Cornet have not been traced.
  Two letter books of John Osborn as envoy
to Dresden 1771-75 were sold at Sotheby's
11 May 1936 lot 153.

OSCOTT, College of St Mary
1870, 1871
First R, xi and App 89-90; Second R,
xiii and App 125-26 [1]

Mostly remain in the archives of the college
at Sutton Coldfield. The Oscott psalter (No 1)
is now British Library Add MS 50000. The
journal of a student in the English College at
Rome (No 15), with Stonor's and Dodd's
collections for the history of English
Catholicism and some other similar material
have been transferred to the Archbishop's
House, Birmingham [NRA 8129].

OSSORY, See of
1885
Tenth R, 44 and App V 219-65 [14]

The Red Book of the diocese of Ossory,
which the Report calendars, remains with
the bishop of Kilkenny. The National Library
of Ireland has microfilm copies (n3672, p3290).

OSWESTRY, Corporation of
1885
Tenth R, 18 and App IV 378 [13]

In Shropshire County Library, Oswestry.

OTHEN, Miss
Midhurst, Sussex. 1872
Third R, xviii and App 277 [2]

No information. Some estate papers were
presented to the Guildford Muniment Room,
Surrey RO in 1950.

OXFORD, Balliol College*
1874
Fourth R, xvii and App 442-51 [3]

At the college in the custody of the bursar.

OXFORD, Corpus Christi College*
1871
Second R, xiv and App 126 [1]

In the college muniment room in the custody
of the librarian [NRA 3705].

OXFORD, Exeter College*
1871
Second R, xiv and App 127-30 [1]

In the college muniment room in the custody
of the keeper of the archives.

OXFORD, Jesus College*
1871-1904
Second R, xv and App 130 [1]; Fifteenth R,
47-49; Sixteenth R, 133;
Welsh MSS II i 1-90 [48]

At the college in the custody of the bursar.
The twenty Welsh MSS were deposited in the
Bodleian Library with the college's other
MS collections in 1886.

OXFORD, Lincoln College*
1871
Second R, xiv and App 130-32 [1]

At the college in the custody of the
archivist. Andrew Clark's transcripts

---

*Most of the reports on the holdings of Oxford colleges deal only with their archives. These, with their
MS collections have been described more recently by P Morgan, Oxford libraries outside the
Bodleian, 2nd edn, Oxford, 1980.*

of many are in the Bodleian Library
(MSS. Top.Oxon.e.82-83, e.97, e.109-15).

OXFORD, Magdalen College*
1874, 1881
Fourth R, xix and App 458-65 [3];
Eighth R, App I 262-69 [7]
At the college in the custody of the archivist
[NRA 20579].

OXFORD, Merton College*
1877
Sixth R, App 545-49 [5]
At the college in the custody of the archivist
[NRA 7626].

OXFORD, New College*
1871
Second R, xiv and App 132-36 [1]
In the college muniment room in the custody
of the librarian and keeper of the archives.
FW Steer, *Archives of New College, Oxford*,
Oxford, 1974.

OXFORD, Oriel College*
1871
Second R, xiv and App 136-37 [1]
At the college in the custody of the treasurer.
The contemporary copy of depositions
taken 1411 (p137b) was reported to be
missing in 1961. CL Shadwell, *Catalogue of
muniments*, 1893-1905.

OXFORD, Pembroke College*
1877
Sixth R, App 549-51 [5]
Remain at the college, the archives and
letter of Charles I (p549) in the muniment
room in the custody of the bursar and the
MSS (pp549-51) in the library.

OXFORD, Queen's College*
1871-77
Second R, xv and App 137-42 [1];
Fourth R, xvii and App 451-58 [3];
Sixth R, App 551-69 [5]
Most of the medieval deeds, including those
relating to God's House, Southampton, have
been deposited in the Bodleian Library
[NRA 1097, vols I, II]. The rest remain at
the college in the custody of the bursar
[NRA 1097, vols III, IV]. Some further deeds
relating to God's House are in
Southampton RO [NRA 13736].

OXFORD, St John's College*
1874
Fourth R, xvii and App 465-68 [3]
At the college in the custody of the librarian
[NRA 7453, 9363].

OXFORD, Trinity College*
1871
Second R, xv and App 142-43 [1]
At the college in the custody of the librarian.
Handlist of selected deeds [NRA 5454].

OXFORD, University College*
1876
Fifth R, xv and App 477-79 [4]
At the college in the custody of the archivist.

OXFORD, Wadham College*
1876
Fifth R, xv and App 479-81 [4]
At the college in the custody of the librarian
[NRA 8127].

OXFORD, Worcester College*
1871
Second R, xv and App 143 [1]
Remain at the college, the archives (p xv) in
the custody of the archivist and the
MS collections (p143) with later
accessions [NRA 10396] in the library.

PALK see Bannatyne

PANTON family
CH Vivian Esq, Plas Gwyn, Anglesey. 1902-05
Fifteenth R, 47-49; Sixteenth R, 134;
Welsh MSS II iii 801-70 [48]
Sold with thirty other MSS to the
National Library of Wales in 1914
(MSS 1970-2068). Other family papers were
bought for the Library by Sir JH Lewis in
1919 (MSS 9051-9107: *Calendar of Wynn
(of Gwydir) papers 1515-1690*, 1926). Further
family and estate papers were bought by
Clwyd RO, Hawarden in 1968 [NRA 16352].

PAPILLON, Lt-Colonel Pelham R
Crowhurst Park, Sussex. 1904
Sixteenth R, 116-17; Various collections
III 256-58 [55]
The certificate and five letters have not been
traced. They are not among the family and

---

*Most of the reports on the holdings of Oxford colleges deal only with their archives. These, with their
MS collections have been described more recently by P Morgan, Oxford libraries outside the
Bodleian, 2nd edn, Oxford, 1980.*

estate papers deposited in Kent AO in 1963 [NRA 18667] nor among the small group of letters and miscellaneous papers given to Northamptonshire RO in 1968 [NRA 21450]. Further family and estate papers have been given to Sussex Archaeological Society and a few deposited by solicitors in Essex RO [NRA 3505] at various dates since 1942.

PARKHAM, Parish of
1874
Fourth R, xviii-xix and App 468-69 [3]

Deposited in Devon RO in 1979 [NRA Devon parish reports] except the church rate book and overseers' books. JI Dredge, *Registers of Parkham*, Devon and Cornwall Record Society, 1906.

PARKINSON, J Lechmere Esq
Ludford House, nr Ludlow, Salop. 1885
Tenth R, 19 and App IV 415-17 [13]

The medieval deeds and most of the other documents were sold to the British Museum in 1894 (Add MSS 34690-91; Add Ch 40792-41412). The historical account of the county of Worcester was deposited in Shropshire RO with other Foxe, Charlton and Wytton family and estate papers from Ludford Park in 1946 [NRA 16218]. The Worcestershire subsidy roll with sixty-three letters from the correspondence (p417) was similarly deposited in 1957 [NRA 11563].

PEAKE, Frederick Esq
Bedford Row, London WC1. 1871, 1872
Second R, xii and App 92-97 [1];
Third R, xvii and App 277-80 [2]

Of the papers of the Nevill family of Holt, the Henry VI roll (pp94, 279-80) was bought by the Bodleian Library, Oxford in 1892 (MS. Eng.hist.b.119). The letters of JB Gastaldi (pp278-79) and some other papers and deeds were bought by the British Museum in 1894 (Add MSS 34679-83; Add Ch 41413-671). Some deeds were presented to the Commission in 1877 and deposited by it in Leicestershire RO in 1954 with additional papers received in 1950 and 1951 [NRA 4351].
The deeds of the Standish family of Standish, Lancs (pp92-93) have not been traced. Other Standish family papers were bought by Lancashire RO from the Portobello Bookshop, London in 1965 [NRA 19738].
   The Commission holds AJ Horwood's transcripts of a number of the papers.

PEMBROKE, Earl of
Wilton House, Wilts. 1884
Ninth R, xvi and App II 379-84 [8]

Remain at Wilton House with other family and estate papers except the Wilton Abbey deeds and rolls (pp379-80) deposited in Wiltshire RO in 1978 [NRA 22080].

PENIARTH see Wynne

PENSHURST see De L'Isle and Dudley

PEPYS MSS see Cambridge, Magdalene College

PERTH, Royal Burgh of
1876
Fifth R, xxi-xxii and App 655 [4]

In Perth and Kinross District Archives.

PERTH, King James's Hospital
1877
Sixth R, xix and App 713-15 [5]

Deposited in the Scottish Record Office, 1957, 1965 (GD 79). *Gifts and Deposits* ii, pp68-69. Typescript inventory.

PETERBOROUGH, Dean and Chapter of
1890, 1891
Twelfth R, 45 and App IX 580-85 [27]

The seven MSS described remain in the cathedral library at Peterborough.
   Most of the capitular estate records have been deposited in Northamptonshire RO at various dates since 1966.

PETWORTH see Leconfield

PETYT see Inner Temple

PHELIPS, W Esq
Montacute House, Somerset. 1870, 1872
First R, ix and App 57-60 [1]; Third R, xviii and App 281-87 [2]

Deposited in or presented to Somerset RO with other family and estate papers at various dates since 1951 [NRA 16738].
The Public Record Office holds transcripts of the Gunpowder Plot MSS (First R, p58: PRO Transcripts 6).

PINE COFFIN, JR Esq
Portledge, Devon. 1874, 1876
Fourth R, xix and App 374-79 [3];
Fifth R, xiv-xv and App 370-86 [4]

Mostly deposited in Devon RO with other
family and estate papers [NRA 19125].

PLEYDELL BOUVERIE, Philip Esq
Brymore, Bridgwater, Somerset. 1885, 1887
Tenth R, 22-23 and App VI 82-98 [15]

The letters and papers of John Pym
presented to the British Museum in 1840
(p82) are now British Library Add MS 11692.
    Most of the other Pym family papers listed
by the Report were later acquired by
Charles Sawyer (*Cat.* Nos 117 (1934) and 155
(1940)). The letters to John Pym and some
items noticed on pp85-96 were subsequently
sold to the Osborn Collection, Beinecke
Library, Yale University (British Library
microfilm RP 456, 628, 641). The letter from
William Rener to Alexander Pym (p95) and
five other documents relating to Bermuda
1632-70 were bought by the Bermuda Archives
in 1944. William Ayshcombe's notebook
(pp82-85) was bought by the Huntington
Library, San Marino in 1955 (HM 30665).
    Some bundles of medieval deeds for
Cannington (p98) were among the Brymore
estate papers acquired in 1942 by Bridgwater
Corporation which gave some of the latter to
Kent AO [NRA 5481] and deposited the
remainder on loan in Somerset RO in 1967
[NRA 21218].
    A few other documents noticed by the
Report were deposited in Somerset RO
[NRA 21218] and Kent AO [NRA 16521] by
solicitors in 1966.
    Fourteen items have remained unaccounted
for since 1940.
See also: Bouverie Pusey; Radnor

PLOWDEN, WF Esq
Plowden Hall, Lydbury North, Salop. 1885
Tenth R, 19 and App IV 409 [13]

Remain at Plowden Hall.

PLYMOUTH, Corporation of
1883, 1885
Ninth R, xiii-xiv and App I 262-84 [8];
Tenth R, 14 and App IV 536-60 [13]

Deposited in West Devon Area RO,
Plymouth. RN Worth, *Calendar of the
Plymouth municipal records*, 1893. CE Welch,
*Guide to the archives department of
Plymouth city libraries, part I, official records*,
1962 and *Plymouth city charters 1439-1935*,
1962. Typescript list of records later than 1835
[NRA 3017].

POLWARTH, Lord
Mertoun House, Berwickshire. 1911-61
Eighteenth R, 106-13; Twenty-First R, 13;
Twenty-Second R, 10; Twenty-Third R, 9;
Twenty-Fourth R, 7; Polwarth I-V [67]

Mostly deposited with other family and
estate papers in the Scottish Record Office at
various dates since 1930 (GD 157).
    The early charters and some other family
papers remain in family possession at Harden,
Hawick [NRA 11011].

PONTEFRACT, Corporation of
1881
Eighth R, xvi and App I 269-76 [7]

Remain in the former municipal offices at
Pontefract, in the care of Wakefield
Archives Department [NRA 5792].

PORTLAND, Duke of
Welbeck Abbey, Notts. 1891-1938
Thirteenth R, 13-26 and App I, II;
Fourteenth R, 11-16 and App II;
Fifteenth R, 8-16 and App IV; Sixteenth R,
14-29; Seventeenth R, 25-28; Nineteenth R,
10-13; Twenty-First R, 13; Portland V-X [29]

The Nalson MSS (Thirteenth R, App I)
were deposited in the Bodleian Library,
Oxford in 1946 (Dep.c.152-76). The
medieval MSS, the charters and the Harley
papers are among the papers placed on loan in
the British Library at various dates since 1947
(MS Loan 29. NRA 20953).
    Further papers of the Dukes of Portland
including some of the Cavendish and Holles
families, Dukes of Newcastle upon Tyne, and
some literary MSS have been deposited in
Nottingham University Library at various
dates since 1949 [NRA 7628]. Estate records
have been deposited in Nottinghamshire RO
[NRA 5959] and in the Scottish Record Office
[NRA 10990] at various dates since 1950.

PORTSMOUTH, Earl of
Hurstbourne Park, Hants. 1881
Eighth R, xi-xii and App I 60-92 [7]

Many of Sir Isaac Newton's papers were sold
at Sotheby's 13 July 1936 (329 lots) when his
accounts ledger (p61) and the three volumes of
his Royal Mint papers (pp63-92) were bought
by Viscount Wakefield and presented to the
Royal Mint (PRO Mint 19/1-5).
    The Newton papers given to Cambridge
University Library in 1872 (Add 3958-4007)
are more fully described in *Catalogue of the
Portsmouth collection of books and papers
written by or belonging to Sir Isaac Newton*,
1888.
    A small group of Wallop family papers is
among the papers of the Jervoise family of
Herriard deposited in Hampshire RO in
1969.

POWIS, Earl of
Powis Castle, Montgomeryshire. 1885
Tenth R, 18 and App IV 378-99 [13]

Robert Barrett's translation of Du Bartas's
poems (p398) was among eighteen
miscellaneous MSS from Powis Castle
library sold at Sotheby's 20 Mar 1923.

The two volumes of letters and papers of
Lord Herbert of Cherbury, the parliamentary
diary and the volume of proceedings against
the Earl of Strafford (pp378-98) were
deposited in the Public Record Office with
other related material in 1956 (PRO 30/53.
NRA 8665).

The papers relating to the county, town and
castle of Montgomery and the genealogical
papers were deposited in the National Library
of Wales in 1959.

Other family and estate papers not noticed
by the Report, including some of the
1st Lord Clive, have been deposited in the
National Library of Wales [NRA 20203,
20151, 23682] and in Shropshire RO
[NRA 11563, 17099] at various dates since
1916. Some further papers of the
1st Lord Clive and the 1st Earl of Powis
were deposited in the India Office Library
and Records in 1956 (MSS Eur G 37).

PRESCOTT, Mrs
Oxford Square, London W. 1871
Second R, xii and App 97-98 [1]

Mostly deposited in Cambridgeshire RO,
Huntingdon in 1962 with other Cromwell
letters and relics [NRA 7584]. Four items
were missing when the collection was
recatalogued in 1960. One of these was
offered for sale by John Wilson in 1978
(*Cat.* 31/18).

PRIDEAUX, Robert Walter Esq
Dartmouth, Devon. 1876
Fifth R, App 423-26 [4]

The thirty-four deeds temp Edw III-Hen IV
have not been accounted for since calendared
by HR Watkin, *Dartmouth, vol I,
Pre-reformation*, Devonshire Association for
the Advancement of Science, Literature and
Art, 1935, pp7-131 passim, as the property of
Mr AM Davson.

PULESTON family Bts
Worthenbury, Flints. 1871-99
Second R, xi and App 65-68 (trustees of the
late Sir Richard Puleston) [1]; Fifteenth R,
39-40 and App VII 307-43 (Revd Sir THG
Puleston) [43]

Mostly deposited in the National Library of
Wales with other family papers in 1921 and
1924 (MSS 3561B-88E, 6704). The
homilies (p65), the 16th cent commonplace
book, John Edwards's memorandum book,

some of the early deeds (p66), the
miscellaneous 16th-17th cent papers relating to
the Civil War in co Denbigh etc (pp67,
307-09) and the letters from Anna Seward
(pp340-43) were given or sold to the
British Museum in 1947 and 1949
(Add MSS 46397-400, 46846;
Add Ch 74370-435).

PYNE, Revd W
Charlton Mackrell and Pitney, Somerset. 1884
Ninth R, xviii and App II, 493-96 [8]

Included among the Combe family papers
deposited in Somerset RO in 1948
[NRA 21217].

QUEEN ANNE'S BOUNTY, Governors of
1881
Eighth R, App I 632-35 [7]

Deposited in the Guildhall Library, London,
1980.

RADNOR, Earl of
Longford Castle, Wilts. 1899
Fifteenth R, 35 and App X 161-72 [47]

The Hungerford family deeds and cartularies
(Nos I-III) are among the Pleydell Bouverie
family and estate papers deposited in
Wiltshire RO at various dates since 1959
[NRA 17343]. The papers relating to Kent
(Nos IV, V) have been deposited in Kent AO
with other papers for the Barony of
Folkestone at various dates since 1950
[NRA 4712]. The volume of Hungerford
family letters (No VI) and the history of
Longford (No VII) remain in family
possession.

Other Pleydell Bouverie family papers
(Coleshill estate) were deposited in 1951 by a
niece of the 5th Earl in Berkshire RO. This
also has the parliamentary papers of the
3rd Earl, bought with Longford Castle by the
National Trust in 1957, and further
Berkshire estate and lieutenancy papers
[NRA 5476].

See also: Bouverie Pusey; Pleydell Bouverie

RAFFLES, Thomas Stamford Esq
Abercromby Square, Liverpool. 1877
Sixth R, xvi and App 468-75 [5]

This large autograph collection was sold in
650 lots at Sotheby's 29 June 1891, when
thirty-seven volumes and eight boxes of
letters were bought by Mrs Rylands
(John Rylands Library, Manchester
University, Eng MSS 343-87). The
remainder have been widely dispersed.

RANYARD, AC Esq
Lincoln's Inn, London WC2. 1876
Fifth R, x and App 404-05 [4]

Dispersed at Sotheby's 4 Dec 1895
lots 547-609.

See also: Webb

RATTRAY, Colonel James
Craighall, Perthshire. 1874
Fourth R, xxiii and App 536-37 [3]

Deposited with other family papers in the
Scottish Record Office in 1981 [NRA 10457]
except the royal letters which were sold at
Sotheby's 20 July 1981 lots 46 and 65.

READING, Corporation of
1887, 1888
Eleventh R, 26-29 and App VII 167-227 [22]

In Reading Central Library.

REYNOLDS, Llywarch Esq
Merthyr Tydfil, Glamorgan. 1902
Welsh MSS II i 372-94 [48]

Sold to the National Library of Wales in 1916
with other Welsh MSS and papers of
Jonathan and Llywarch Reynolds
(MSS 970-97).

RICHMOND AND LENNOX, Duke of
Gordon Castle, Morayshire. 1870
First R, xii and App 114-16 [1]

The letters noticed on p115a were deposited
in West Sussex RO in 1965. See *The
Goodwood estate archives* ii, 1972, pp11-12, 95.
The remainder have been presented to the
Scottish Record Office with other papers from
Gordon Castle (GD 44). *Gifts and Deposits* ii,
pp4-11 and typescript inventory.

RIDGWAY, Matthew Esq
Dewsbury, Yorks. 1874
Fourth R, App 404-05 [3]

The three volumes listed have not been
traced.

RINUCCINI MS see Leicester, Earl of

RIPON, Marquess of
Studley Royal, Yorks. 1876, 1877
Fifth R, vii and App 294 [4]; Sixth R,
xi and App 243-50 [5]

Following the death of the 2nd Marquess of
Ripon in 1923 Studley Royal passed to
his cousin Commander CG Vyner.

Two MS books included in the sale of the
library through Kemp 12 June 1925 are now

in the Bodleian Library, Oxford (MS. Lyell 2:
St Jerome's letters p249) and the Folger
Library, Washington (MS 2075.2:
Queen Elizabeth's proclamations p250).

The Fountains Abbey records (p249) and
about one third of the other MS books noticed
were bought by Leeds Archives Department
in 1981 with other estate records and family
papers [NRA 6160]. The Lilium medicine
(Fifth R) is British Library Add MS 62131.

No information has been obtained about
the remaining MS books which are thought to
have been destroyed in a fire at Studley Royal
in 1946.

The papers of the 1st Earl and 1st Marquess
of Ripon were presented to the British
Museum in 1923 (Add MSS 40862-80,
43510-644).

See also: Cowper, Countess

ROCHESTER, Corporation of
1883
Ninth R, ix and App I 286-89 [8]

Remain at Rochester Guildhall [NRA 9386].

ROCHESTER BRIDGE,
Wardens and Assistants of
1883
Ninth R, ix and App I 285-86 [8]

Remain with the bridge clerk, 18 Star Hill,
Rochester. *Rochester Bridge Trust and the
New College of Cobham*, 1954.
Some 19th-20th cent legal papers were
deposited in 1954 in Kent AO [NRA 6345]
and Essex RO [NRA 22417].

ROGERS, JJ Esq
Penrose, Helston, Cornwall. 1871, 1874
Second R, xii and App 98-99 [1];
Fourth R, xv and App 405-06 [3]

Mostly remain at Penrose but not open for
research [NRA 5033]. The ten volumes of
sermons of John Bishop (Fourth R, p405b)
are in the Osborn Collection, Beinecke
Library, Yale University (MS b 244/1-11).

ROLLO, Lord
Duncrub Park, Dunning, Perthshire. 1872
Third R, xxiii and App 406-07 [2]

The charters and Montrose letter were
presented with other family papers to the
Scottish Record Office in 1946 (GD 56).
Gifts and Deposits ii, pp47-48. Typescript
inventory.

The letters of the 5th Lord Rollo were
presented to the British Museum in the same
year (Add MS 46196). The patent of peerage
and the 5th Lord Rollo's commission remain
in family possession.

ROSS, George Esq
Pitcalnie, Rossshire. 1877
Sixth R, xix and App 715-19 [5]

Presented with other family papers to the Scottish Record Office at various dates since 1957 (GD 199).

ROSSE, Earl of
Birr Castle, Parsonstown, co Offaly. 1870, 1871
First R, xii and App 127-28; Second R, xx and App 217-23 [1]

Remain at Birr Castle, where a number of the earlier documents described by the First Report were destroyed in a fire. The National Library of Ireland has microfilms of some of the Irish correspondence and papers.

ROSSLYN, Earl of
Dysart House, Kirkcaldy, Fife. 1871
Second R, xviii and App 191-92 [1]

The deeds and papers noticed were sold to RGE Wemyss in 1896. Most are now at Wemyss Castle but not open for research.

The 1st Earl's American papers were sold to William L Clements in 1929 and are in the William L Clements Library, University of Michigan [NRA 22710]. The letters from the Duke of Portland were returned to his family and are now among the Portland papers deposited in Nottingham University Library [NRA 7628].

Estate papers from the Dysart Estates Office were deposited in the Scottish Record Office in 1961 (GD 164). A volume of documents relating to the burgh of Dysart was deposited in Kirkcaldy Museum and Art Gallery in the same year [NRA 18847].

See also: Wemyss

ROTHES, Countess of
Leslie House, Fife. 1874
Fourth R, xx-xxi and App 492-511 [3]

Deposited with other family papers in the Scottish Record Office at various dates since 1952 (GD 204). Typescript inventory [Partial list NRA 14868]. Further papers were deposited there by Shepherd and Wedderburn WS of Edinburgh in 1966 (GD 242).

ROUND, James Esq
Birch Hall, Essex. 1895, 1896
Fourteenth R, 38-39 and App IX 267-366 [38]

Mostly among the Round and Gray family papers given to Essex RO at various dates between 1944 and 1964 [Partial list NRA 20947]. *Guide to the Essex RO*, 1969, pp113-17. The deed of the Earl of Warwick 1465 (p270) and the Petkum papers (pp317-66) are in the British Library

(Add Ch 74449; Add MS 46489A,B). Nine items including Charles Gray's parliamentary note-book 1747 (pp309-17) have not been accounted for.

Some papers and correspondence of JH Round, the historian, are in London University Library [NRA 20042].

ROXBURGHE, Duke of
Floors Castle, Kelso, Roxburghshire. 1894, 1895
Fourteenth R, 46-47 and App III 1-55 [34]

Mostly remain at Floors Castle [NRA 10542]. The charter of Malcolm IV to Kelso Abbey (No 75) was deposited in the National Library of Scotland in 1941.

ROYAL COLLEGE OF PHYSICIANS OF LONDON
1881
Eighth R, xiv and App I 226-35 [7]

Remain at the college in the custody of the librarian. HM Barlow, *Descriptive catalogue of the legal and other documents in the archives of the Royal College of Physicians of London*, typescript, 1924.
Ker, *Medieval MSS* i, pp196-228.

ROYAL INSTITUTION
1904-19
Seventeenth R, 103-09; Eighteenth R, 137-44; Royal Institution I-IV [59]

The Institution's American MSS are now in the Public Record Office (PRO 30/55, Carleton Papers) by gift, in 1957, of Her Majesty the Queen to whom they were presented in that year by the Colonial Williamsburg Foundation, Virginia. The papers were bought for Colonial Williamsburg by John D Rockefeller Jr in 1930. Photographic copies are held by New York Public Library and at Williamsburg. The British Library has transcripts (Add MSS 42257-496).

RUTHERFORD, William Oliver Esq
Edgerston, Jedburgh, Roxburghshire. 1879
Seventh R, xvi and App 735-37 [6]

Bought in 1980 by the National Library of Scotland (Acc 7676) which in the same year also acquired some other family papers by transfer from the Scottish Record Office.

RUTLAND, Duke of
Belvoir Castle, Leics. 1870-1907
First R, x and App 10-12 [1]; Twelfth R, 13-23 and App IV, V; Fourteenth R, 6-11 and App I; Seventeenth R, 19-25; Rutland IV [24]

Remain at Belvoir Castle. Not normally open for research.

RYE, Corporation of
1876, 1892
Fifth R, xvii and App 488-516 [4];
Thirteenth R, 51-55 and App IV 1-246 [31]

Deposited in East Sussex RO, 1955.
RF Dell, *Records of Rye corporation,*
Lewes, 1962.

SACKVILLE, Lord
Knole, Kent. 1874-1906
Fourth R, xiii-xiv and App 276-317 (Earl
De La Warr) [3]; Seventh R, xiii and
App 249-60 [6]; Twenty-Second R, 11;
Twenty-Third R, 9; Sackville I, II [80]

Mostly deposited in Kent AO with other
family and estate papers of the Sackville,
Whitworth and Cranfield families [NRA 8575].

See also: Stopford Sackville

ST ALBANS, Corporation of
1876
Fifth R, xviii and App 565-68 [4]

In the custody of the chief executive,
St Albans City Council [NRA 3023].

ST ANDREWS, University of
1871
Second R, xx and App 206-09 [1]

Remain at St Andrews University Library in
the care of the keeper of MSS.

ST AUDRIES see Hood

ST GERMANS, Earl of
Port Eliot, Cornwall. 1870
First R, x and App 41-44 [1]
Remain at Port Eliot.

SALISBURY, Bishop of
1907
Seventeenth R, 109-12; Various collections IV,
1-12 [55]

Deposited with other episcopal and
archidiaconal records in Wiltshire RO.
P Stewart, *Guide to the records of the bishop,
the archdeacons of Salisbury and
Wiltshire . . .* , 1973.

SALISBURY, Dean and Chapter of
1870-1904
First R, x and App 90-91 [1]; Sixteenth R,
102; Various collections I 338-88 [55]

Remain at Salisbury. The papers noticed by
the First Report are now MS 189 in the
cathedral library. Access to the rest is through
the cathedral librarian.

SALISBURY, Corporation of
1907
Seventeenth R, 122-23; Various collections
IV 191-254 [55]

Remain in the Salisbury District Council
Muniment Room in the care of Wiltshire RO.

SALISBURY, Marquess of
Hatfield House, Herts. 1870-1976
Third R, xii-xiii and App 147-80 [2];
Fourth R, xii and App 199-227 [3]; Fifth R,
vii and App 261-94 [4]; Sixth R,
App 250-77 [5]; Seventh R, xiii and
App 182-96 [6]; Twelfth R, 23-34;
Thirteenth R, 26-31; Fourteenth R, 16-23;
Fifteenth R, 21-27; Sixteenth R, 48-56;
Seventeenth R, 28-34; Eighteenth R, 34-57;
Nineteenth R, 9-10; Twenty-First R, 12;
Twenty-Second R, 10; Twenty-Third R, 8;
Salisbury (Cecil) I-XXIV [9]

Remain at Hatfield House. Access through
the librarian/archivist. The British Library
has microfilms of the Cecil papers
(M/485(1)-(127)). There is a typescript
calendar of the correspondence of the
3rd Marquess as Foreign Secretary
[NRA 9226].

SALWEY, Alfred Esq
Overton, Salop. 1885
Tenth R, 19 and App IV 409-15 [13]

Remain in family possession at the Lodge,
Ludlow except the diary of the
Restoration Parliament 1660 (p410)
deposited in the Bodleian Library, Oxford
in 1938 (MS.Dep.f.9).
  Some other manorial and estate records
from Richards Castle and Moor Park have
been deposited in Shropshire RO at various
dates since 1957 [NRA 11563].

SANDWICH, Corporation of
1876
Fifth R, xviii-xix and App 568-71 [4]
Deposited in Kent AO, 1956 [NRA 3678].

SAVILE, Augustus William Esq
Rufford Abbey, Notts. 1887, 1888
Eleventh R, 24 and App VII 119-26 [22]
Mostly deposited in Nottinghamshire RO at
various dates since 1957 with other family and

estate papers [NRA 6119]. The Rufford Abbey cartulary (p119) was placed on loan in the British Museum in 1954 (MS Loan 41; transcript in Harleian MS 1063).

Other Yorkshire estate papers (cf p126) have been placed in Dewsbury Central Library at various dates since 1969 or retained in the Thornhill Estate Office [NRA 14864].

SEAFIELD, Earl of
Cullen House, Banffshire. 1872-95
Third R, xxii-xxiii and App 403-04 [2];
Fourteenth R, 50-51 and App III 191-238 [34]

Deposited with other family papers in the Scottish Record Office at various dates since 1956 (GD 248).

SELKIRK, Earl of
St Mary's Isle, Kirkcudbrightshire. 1874
Fourth R, xxiii and App 516-18 [3]

Following the death of the Earl of Selkirk in 1885 the Lanarkshire papers apparently passed to the 12th Duke of Hamilton. The 4th Earl of Haddington's household account book was among the papers at St Mary's Isle destroyed in a fire in 1940. The papers which survive remain in family possession [Partial list NRA 10180].

SEMPILL see Forbes, Sir William Bt

SEWELL, Revd WH see Yaxley

SHAFTESBURY, Earl of
St Giles, Dorset. 1872
Third R, xi and App 216-17 [2]

The items noticed were presented to the Public Record Office in 1871 (PRO 30/24. NRA 23640).

Other family papers remaining at St Giles are not open for research. Some papers of the 7th Earl are among the Palmerston papers in the possession of the Broadlands Archives Trust [NRA 12889]. A small group of Dorchester deeds was deposited in Dorset RO in 1969 [NRA 16912].

SHAW STEWART see Stewart, Sir MR Shaw Bt

SHERREN, James Esq
Weymouth, Dorset. 1876
Fifth R, App 576-90 [4]

The papers relating to the corporation of Weymouth and Melcombe Regis are now in the custody of Weymouth and Portland Borough Council. Access through the curator, Weymouth Museum.

SHIRLEY, Evelyn Philip Esq
Ettington Hall, Warwicks. 1876
Fifth R, x and App 362-69 [4]

Mostly dispersed with other family papers after a private sale to ASW Rosenbach in 1929 and a sale by auction at Sotheby's 29 Apr 1947 lots 257-348 passim. Eventual recipients include the Rosenbach Museum and Library, Philadelphia (Nos 6, 40: Rosenbach 232/11,14), the Folger Library, Washington (Nos 7, 9: MSS G.b.4, Add 670), Keele University Library (No 55: Raymond Richards collection no 32), and the Bodleian Library (No 56: MS.Top.gen.a.9).

The papers remaining in family possession at Ormly Hall, Isle of Man include Nos 14, 19, 24, 37, 39, 71, 76, 85 and 97 [NRA 7573]. The rental 1657-65 (p369) is among other Ettington estate papers deposited in Warwickshire RO at various dates since 1952 [NRA 17508].

The family's Irish estate papers, noticed in 'NLI report on private collections, no 142', *Analecta Hibernica*, xx, 1958, pp259-78, were deposited in the Public Record Office of Northern Ireland in 1981.

Related family and estate papers of the Earls Ferrers are held by Leicestershire RO [NRA 0874], Staffordshire RO [NRA 7148] and the William Salt Library, Stafford [NRA 7149].

SHREWSBURY, Corporation of
1899
Fifteenth R, 42-43 and App X 1-65 [47]

Deposited in Shropshire RO, 1975 except the royal charters and burgess rolls retained at Shrewsbury Guildhall. *Calendar of the muniments and records of the borough of Shrewsbury*, Shrewsbury, 1896.

SHREWSBURY, Earl of
1870-1904
First R, xi and App 50 (Executors of 17th Earl of Shrewsbury) [1]; Sixteenth R, 107-08; Various collections II 289-336 (Lord Edmund Talbot, 1st Viscount Fitzalan of Derwent) [55]

Sold to the British Museum in 1947 with other papers of the second line of the Talbot family Earls of Shrewsbury (Add MSS 46454-64; Add Ch 72121-74194).

For the dispersal and locations of papers of the senior male Talbot line which passed on the death of the 8th Earl of Shrewsbury in 1617 to Henry Howard, 6th Duke of Norfolk, see FW Steer, *Arundel Castle archives* i-ii, 1968, 1972, and the introduction to HMC *Bath V*, 1981, with references there cited.

Other Talbot and Chetwynd family papers, deriving from descendants of Sir John Talbot of Salwarpe, ancestor of the 3rd Earl Talbot, afterwards 18th Earl of Shrewsbury, were deposited in or transferred to Staffordshire RO between 1962 and 1978 [NRA 8481]. Smaller deposits have been placed in Hereford and Worcester RO, Worcester [NRA 1489], the William Salt Library, Stafford [NRA 7274, 7275], Berkshire RO [NRA 0098], the Bodleian Library, Oxford [NRA 0097], and Shropshire RO [NRA 11563] at various dates since 1949.

SKRINE, Henry Duncan Esq
Claverton Manor, Somerset. 1887
Eleventh R, 24 and App I [16]

Mr Heath Wilson's translations, which the Report printed, of Amerigo Salvetti's despatches from London to Florence 1625-28 have not been found. The original despatches remain in the Archivio di Stato, Florence and there are transcripts of them in the British Library (Add MS 27962A-W).

SMITH, Philip Vernon Esq
Lincoln's Inn, London WC2. 1890, 1891
Twelfth R, 42-43 and App IX, 343-74 [27]

The papers of Joseph Smith, private secretary to William Pitt the younger, remain in family possession. Microfilm copies are held by the Library of Congress, Washington (*Checklist* F 217-18).

SNEYD, Revd Walter
Keele Hall, Staffs. 1872
Third R, xvii and App 287-90 [2]

Dispersed with the rest of Walter Sneyd's MS collections at Sotheby's 16 Dec 1903 (866 lots), 28 Nov 1927 lots 315, 375, 474, 27 June 1932 lots 129-98, 23 Apr 1934 lots 133-72 and at Hodgson's 26 Mar 1929 lots 1-290 passim.

The numerous Sneyd and Canonici MSS that can now be traced include only a few described by the Report, namely British Library Add MS 36880, Bodleian Library MS.Fr.d.16, and one each in the Folger Library, Washington, the Pierpont Morgan Library, New York, and the Beinecke Library, Yale University.

Other Sneyd family and estate papers were bought by Keele University in 1957 [NRA 1248].

SOMERSET, County of
1872, 1879
Third R, xix and App 333-34 [2]; Seventh R, xv and App 693-701 [6]

In Somerset RO. *Interim handlist of Somerset quarter sessions documents and other official records*, 1947.

SOMERSET, Duke of
Maiden Bradley, Wilts. 1898, 1899
Fifteenth R, 16-18 and App VII 1-151 [43]

The 16th cent correspondence (pp7-51) descended to Sir William Pennington Ramsden Bt and was deposited with the papers of the 12th Duke of Somerset in Devon RO in 1967 [NRA 12798]. Most of the remainder were deposited in Wiltshire RO in 1977 with other family papers.

Manorial and estate records from Berry Pomeroy were deposited in Wiltshire RO in 1952 [NRA 2604] and by solicitors in Devon RO in 1965 [NRA 8073]. Papers from Bulstrode Park were deposited by Sir William Pennington Ramsden in Buckinghamshire RO in 1962 [NRA 11704].

See also: Bath; Muncaster

SOUTHAMPTON, Corporation of
1887
Eleventh R, 29-33 and App III 1-144 [18]

In Southampton RO. *Southampton records: Guide to the records of the corporation and absorbed authorities . . .* , 1964, and typescript supplements [NRA 4905]. There is also a separate typescript list of the Molyneux papers (pp31-40. NRA 4957).

SOUTHAMPTON, God's House
see Oxford, Queen's College

SOUTHESK, Earl of
Kinnaird Castle, Angus. 1879
Seventh R, xvi and App 716-26 [6]

Remain at Kinnaird Castle [NRA 10554]. Some American papers of Andrew Elliot 1766-87 not reported on were sold to New York State Library, Albany in 1953.

SOUTHWARK, Catholic Bishop of
1872
Third R, xxi and App 233-37 [2]

Most of the items listed on p233 and at the head of p234 are now at Stonyhurst College, Lancs. The copies of Weldon's Collections and Chronological notes are at Downside Abbey, Somerset. The remaining documents have been merged with other series of papers in Westminster Diocesan Archives, except the letters and papers 1575-1688 (pp234-35) which are kept there separately as Stonyhurst Anglia A VIII, IX.

Access to the Southwark Catholic diocesan records is through Archbishop's House, Southwark.

SOUTHWELL MINSTER
1890, 1891
Twelfth R, 46 and App IX 539-45 [27]

Most of the muniments and MS books remain in the minster library [NRA 7879]. The court rolls, wills, registers of wills and papists' records (pp542-45) have been transferred to Nottinghamshire RO which also holds other capitular and prebendal estate records deposited by the Church Commissioners and the stewards of chapter manors.

SOUTHWOLD, Corporation of
1914, 1919
Eighteenth R, 218-20; Various collections VII 114-18 [55]

Remain at Southwold in the custody of Waveney District Council [NRA 3026].

SPENCER, Earl
Spencer House, London SW. 1871
Second R, ix-x and App 12-20 [1]

Remain in family possession at Althorp, Northants but not open for research. A general description of the collection by the 7th Earl Spencer is printed in *Bulletin of the National Register of Archives*, xiii, 1964, pp21-26. Other 18th-19th cent family papers at Althorp are listed by JS Corbett and HW Richmond, *Private papers of George, 2nd Earl Spencer, first lord of the admiralty, 1794-1801*, Navy Records Society xlvi, xlviii, lviii, lix, 4 vols, 1913-24 and in NRA 10410.

A few MSS not noticed by the Report were sold with the Althorp Library to Mrs Rylands in 1892 and are now in the John Rylands Library, Manchester University (Eng MSS 47-49, 52-53, 62-72, 74).

STAFFORD, Lord
Costessy Hall, Norfolk. 1885
Tenth R, 25 and App IV 152-68 [13]

The MSS were divided in 1913 after the death of the 11th Lord Stafford, when over half of them passed to Sir William Henry Stafford Jerningham Bt and were later given to Norfolk RO [NRA 4643] apart from a few items retained by his grandson Mr A Murray [NRA 0080].

The remainder were taken by the 12th Lord Stafford to Swynnerton Park and subsequently deposited in Staffordshire RO in 1961 with other family papers. [Partial list NRA 9561]. The Revd JB Frith's lists and notes of these are now in the William Salt Library, Stafford [NRA 5924, 8511].

Two account rolls of the Duke of Gloucester 1392 and the 3rd Duke of Buckingham 1503-04, not noticed by the Report, were presented to the British Museum in 1923 (Add MS 40859A,B). Some other medieval estate papers for Thornbury, Gloucestershire

were given by the 12th Lord Stafford to Major Sir Algar Howard and have since been deposited in Gloucestershire RO [NRA 14347].

STAIR, Earl of
Oxenfoord Castle, Dalkeith, Midlothian. 1871
Second R, viii and App 188-91 [1]

Deposited with other family papers in the Scottish Record Office, 1965 (GD 135. NRA 10017).

STAUNTON, HC Esq
Staunton Hall, Notts. 1914, 1919
Eighteenth R, 229-30; Various collections VII 360-75 [55]

Remain in family possession at Staunton Hall with other papers [NRA 8289].

Some other family and estate papers were deposited in Nottinghamshire RO in 1950 [NRA 6871].

STEWART, Sir MR Shaw Bt
Ardgowan, Greenock, Renfrewshire. 1874
Fourth R, xxiii and App 528 [3]

Some of the title deeds noticed by the Report are among the papers from Ardgowan Estate Office deposited in Strathclyde Regional Archives in 1975 [NRA 14672].

Some writs 1442-1878 were presented to the Scottish Record Office by Messrs Shepherd & Wedderburn WS, Edinburgh in 1959 (GD 242).

STEWART, Captain James
Alltyrodyn, Llandyssil, Cardiganshire. 1885
Tenth R, 5-8 and App IV 59-146 [13]

Sold at Sotheby's 29 Nov 1901 (318 lots) with other papers of the Moore family of Bankhall.

Most of the correspondence and the Lancashire and Cheshire deeds (1,368 documents) are now in Liverpool RO with additional family papers bought in 1932 and 1964 [NRA 18447]. 123 miscellaneous documents are now in the Sydney Jones Library, Liverpool University with other family papers bought in 1967. Both groups were listed by J Brownbill and K Walker, *Calendar of . . . deeds and papers of the Moore family of Bankhall*, Lancashire and Cheshire Record Society, lxvii, 1913.

Eventual recipients of other parts of the collection include Lord Derby (21 lots relating to the Stanley family), the Duke of Rutland (13 lots of miscellaneous autograph letters, through Captain CL Lindsay), Wirral Archives (3 lots including some letters noticed on pp91, 96. NRA 8635), Suffolk RO, Bury St Edmunds (10 lots including some letters noticed on pp126-27, 141, through

Captain ES Bence. NRA 6826),
Leicestershire RO (letters relating to
Appleby Grammar School pp138-40.
NRA 6952) and Cambridge University Library
(fragments of a court roll and rental p60:
Add 4442-43).

STIRLING, Miss Mary Eleanor
Renton House, Coldingham, Berwickshire.
1876
Fifth R, xxi and App 646-50 [4]

Remained in family possession in 1908. No
subsequent information.

STIRLING MAXWELL, Sir John Bt
Keir House, Dunblane, Perthshire. 1885
Tenth R, 34-37 and App I 58-81 [10]

Deposited with other family and estate papers
from Keir and Pollok in Strathclyde Regional
Archives at various dates since 1969
[NRA 24669].

A few other papers have been deposited by
Dundas & Wilson CS, Edinburgh in the
Scottish Record Office (GD 236).

STONYHURST COLLEGE
1871-85
Second R, xiii and App 143-46 [1]; Third R,
xxi and App 334-41 [2]; Tenth R, 25 and
App IV 176-99 [13]

Remain at Stonyhurst College, Lancs
[NRA 22957], apart from six missing MSS,
the Stonyhurst Gospel (p334) now in the
British Library (MS Loan 74), and the papers
relating to the Pole family which have been
returned to Mount St Mary's College, Derbys.

See also: Southwark

STOPFORD SACKVILLE, Mrs
Drayton House, Northants. 1884-1919
Ninth R, xx-xxi and App III [8]; Sixteenth R,
110-11; Eighteenth R, 135-37; Stopford
Sackville I, II [49]

The papers calendared in Sackville I
(Sections IV, V, IX-XI, XIII, XVII) and
Sackville II were sold with related papers to
William L Clements in 1927 and are now
in the William L Clements Library, University
of Michigan. RG Adams, *The papers of
Lord George Germain*, Ann Arbor, 1928.
*Guide to the MS collections in the
William L Clements Library*, 1942. The rest of
the material noticed remains at Drayton
House.

Some other deeds and estate papers have
been deposited in Northamptonshire RO
[NRA 6280].

STORY MASKELYNE, Nevil Esq
Bassett Down House, Wroughton, Wilts. 185
Tenth R, 8-9 and App IV 146-52 [13]

The Proger letters were sold at Sotheby's
2 July 1968 lots 410-23. Ten of the letters
from Lord Cottington are now in the
Osborn Collection, Beinecke Library, Yale
University (British Library microfilm
RP 278(3)).

Some other papers of the Story Maskelyne
and Arnold Foster families were deposited in
Wiltshire RO in 1977 [NRA 23462].

STRACHEY, Sir Edward Bt
Sutton Court, Pensford, Somerset. 1877
Sixth R, xiv-xv and App 395-407 [5]

The papers of John Strachey (pp395-96) and
the Kirkpatrick correspondence (pp404-07)
are included among the family and estate
papers deposited in or bequeathed to Somerset
RO at various dates since 1949 [NRA 4321].

The Indian papers of Edward Strachey
(p407), John Carnac (p398) and the
2nd Lord Clive (p398) with some of those of
Sir Henry Strachey Bt and the 1st Lord Clive
(pp396-98) were sold in 1965 to the India
Office Library and Records (MSS Eur F 128).
Some papers of Sir Richard Strachey not
listed by the Report were also deposited there
in the same year by James Strachey
(MSS Eur F 127).

Henry Strachey's American papers
(pp399-404) have not been traced apart from
the loyalists' memorial (p401) sold privately to
the New York Historical Society in 1947.
Some related papers sold at Sotheby's
13 Nov 1922 lot 396 and 3 July 1967 lot 242
were bought by the William L Clements
Library, University of Michigan
[NRA 24303]. Others are in the Library of
Congress, Washington [NRA 24302].

STRATFORD UPON AVON, Corporation of
1883
Ninth R, xiv and App I 289-93 [8]

In the Shakespeare Birthplace Trust RO,
Stratford upon Avon.

STRATHMORE, Earl of
Glamis Castle, Angus. 1871-95
Second R, xviii-xix and App 185-86 [1];
Fourteenth R, 49-50 and App III 174-90 [34]

Remain at Glamis Castle [NRA 0381].
Another group of Bowes family papers from
Streatlam Castle, sold at Sotheby's 26 Mar
1923 lots 646-91, is described and listed by
BLH Horn and FJ Shaw, 'Bowes bound
correspondence and papers', *Archives*,
xiv, no 63, Spring 1980, pp134-40.

STRICKLAND, Walter Charles Esq
Sizergh Castle, Westmorland. 1876
Fifth R, ix-x and App 329-32 [4]

Remain at Sizergh Castle. Access through
Cumbria RO, Kendal.

STUART, Hon Henry Constable Maxwell
Traquair House, Innerleithen, Peeblesshire.
1884
Ninth R, xviii-xix and App II 241-62 [8]

Remain at Traquair House [NRA 9765].

STUART, Alexander Charles Esq
Eaglescarnie, Haddington, E Lothian. 1881
Eighth R, xvii-xviii and App I 310-15 [7]

Sold to the Faculty of Advocates in 1923 and
transferred in 1925 to the National Library of
Scotland (Adv MSS 23.3.26-30).

STUART MSS
Windsor Castle, Berks. 1902-26
Sixteenth R, 12-14; Seventeenth R, 13-19;
Eighteenth R, 102-06; Nineteenth R, 22-25;
Stuart I-VII [56]

Remain in The Royal Archives, Windsor.
Access restricted. London University Library
holds microfilm copies and an index.

SUTHERLAND, Duke of
Dunrobin Castle, Sutherland and Trentham,
Staffs. 1871, 1876
Second R, xvi-xvii and App 177-80 [1];
Fifth R, vi-vii and App 135-214 [4]

The Dunrobin MSS were deposited in the
National Library of Scotland in 1980
[Summary list NRA 11006].
　　Ten volumes of Trentham MSS were
added to the family papers deposited in
Staffordshire RO in 1966 [NRA 10699].
Other family papers and estate records have
been deposited at various dates since 1955 in
the William Salt Library, Stafford
[NRA 7816] and in Shropshire RO
[NRA 11563]. The Lilleshall cartulary was
sold to the British Museum in 1959
(Add MS 50121).
　　Some further MSS from Trentham not
listed by the Reports were sold at Sotheby's
19 Nov 1906 and at Christie's 2 July 1975.
Colonel RJ Gordon's South African journals,
sold at Christie's 4 Apr 1979 lot 73 are now in
the Brenthurst Library, Johannesburg.

SYON see Northumberland

TALBOT DE MALAHIDE, Lord
Malahide Castle, co Dublin. 1870, 1881
First R, xii and App 128 [1]; Eighth R, xviii
and App I 493-99 [7]

The poem on Irish affairs temp James II
(First R, No 3), the 1689 correspondence and
the 1447 exemplification (Eighth R, pp493-97)
have not been traced. The remaining items are
among the family and estate papers given to
the Bodleian Library, Oxford in 1977.

TENTERDEN, Corporation of
1877
Sixth R, App 569-72 [5]

Deposited in Kent AO in 1954 apart from a
few items retained at the Town Hall
[NRA 4341].

THETFORD, Corporation of
1914, 1919
Eighteenth R, 220-25; Various collections
VII 119-52 [55]

At King's House, Thetford. Access through
Norfolk RO.

THROCKMORTON, Sir N William Bt
Coughton Court, Warwick and Buckland
House, Berks. 1872, 1885
Third R, xxi and App 256-58 (Coughton) [2];
Tenth R, 25-26 and App IV 168-76
(Buckland) [13]

Mostly remain at Coughton Court, in the
custody of the National Trust [NRA 0741].
　　The Buckland missal was sold privately in
1909, resold at Sotheby's 13 Dec 1932 lot 293
and presented in 1933 by Sir John Noble Bt to
the Bodleian Library, Oxford (MS. Don.b.5).
The other medieval devotional MSS
(Tenth R, p171) were sold at Christie's
20 Dec 1972 lots 204-11 passim.
　　The manorial records and some later deeds
have been deposited in the Shakespeare
Birthplace Trust RO, Stratford upon Avon at
various dates since 1936. Typescript list.
　　Some other Buckland manorial records,
deeds and estate papers were deposited in
Berkshire RO in 1964 [NRA 11515]. Estate
maps and plans of Coughton Court 17th-20th
cent were deposited in Warwickshire RO in
1980.

TIGHE, KB Esq
Woodstock, Inistioge, co Kilkenny. 1909, 1919
Eighteenth R, 135; Various collections VI
435-37 [55]

The items noticed have not been seen since
1939.
　　Some other family papers were acquired by
the National Library of Ireland in 1951 and
1954 [NRA 24616].

TILLARD, P Edward Esq
The Holme, Hunts. 1899
Fifteenth R, 42 and App X 78-91 [47]

Remain in family possession at Tunbridge
Wells, Kent.

TOLLEMACHE, John Esq, 1st Baron
Tollemache
Helmingham Hall, Suffolk. 1870
First R, x and App 60-61 [1]

Almost all dispersed by private sales 1953-56
or by auction at Sotheby's 16 May 1955
lots 118-19, 6 June 1961 lots 1-23,
14 June 1965 lots 1-38, 29 Apr 1969
lots 279-83, 9 July 1969 lot 32, 8 July 1970
lots 62-69, 12 July 1971 lots 38-41.
    The Orosius (p60a) and the works of
SS Augustine and Ambrose from
St Osyth Abbey (p61b) are now British
Library Add MSS 47967, 56252.
    The treatise Of Maumetrie (p60a), the
latin grammatical treatise (p61a), and a
commentary on the Pauline Epistles (p61b) are
Bodleian Library MSS.Eng.th.f.39,
Lat.misc.e.108, Lat.th.c.28.
    The latin treatises on the Decalogue (p60b)
are in London University Library and a
commentary of Rabanus Maurus in the
Picton Library, Liverpool.
    Trevisa's translation (p60a), Lydgate's Troy
and Sir Gennerides (p60b), a 'splendid' Bible
(p61b), and St Ambrose De Officiis are in the
Pierpont Morgan Library, New York.
    Six MSS, including the Trial of the Earl of
Essex, the sermons of St Augustine (p61b),
and the herbal and medical tracts (p61b) are in
the Huntington Library, San Marino.
    Single MSS are in the Osborn Collection,
Beinecke Library, Yale University, in
Princeton University Library (Chaucer's
poems, p61b) and the Watson Library,
University of Kansas, Lawrence.
    Microfilm copies of seventeen MSS that
have been exported are held by the British
Library.
    Other family and estate papers remain at
Helmingham Hall. Some estate papers have
also been deposited by solicitors in Suffolk RO,
Ipswich [NRA 6277].
    The related papers of the Tollemache
family, baronets and Earls of Dysart are now
kept at Buckminster Park [NRA 23003]. The
Ham House estate papers were deposited in
Surrey RO in 1953 [NRA 17204].

TORPHICHEN, Lord
Calder House, Midlothian. 1871
Second R, xix and App 196 [1]

Deposited in the Scottish Record Office, 1951
(GD 119). Typescript inventory.

TORRENS, WT McCullagh Esq
1871
Second R, xv and App 99-100 [1]

The thirty-seven volumes of debates in the
Irish House of Commons were bought at
Sotheby's 22 Dec 1898 with forty-five other
volumes by the Library of Congress,
Washington (MS 62.4531). The Public Record
Office of Northern Ireland holds microfilm
copies.

TOTNES, Corporation of
1872
Third R, xx and App 341-50 [2]

Deposited in Devon RO at various dates
since 1967 [NRA 19650].

TOWNELEY, Colonel
Towneley Hall, Lancs. 1874
Fourth R, xvi-xvii and App 406-16, 613-14 [3]

Dispersed with other Towneley family papers
at Sotheby's, 18 June (10 lots) and 27 June
1883 (241 lots) or in later private sales.
Twenty-nine of the lots offered at auction
were withdrawn or bought in by Charles
Towneley's sons-in-law Lord Norreys,
later 7th Earl of Abingdon, and the
1st Lord O'Hagan.
    Of the forty-nine original MSS noticed by
the Report, Nos 1, 10, 14 are in the British
Library (Add MSS 32097-98, 32101),
Nos 2, 34 in the Farrer collection in
Manchester City Archives Department
[NRA 17338], No 3 in the Chambers
collection in Leeds Archives Department
[NRA 19413], Nos 6, 8 in the Bodleian
Library, No 18 in Burnley Central Library,
Nos 22 (Robert Nowell's executorship
accounts), 23, 25 in Chetham's Library,
Manchester, and part of No 31 in
Cambridge University Library.
    Of the 17th cent transcripts the British
Library has fifteen (Add MSS 32099-115
passim), Manchester City Archives Department
has eleven, Chetham's Library has nine
(33671-73, 33675, 33677, 33679-82), Leeds
Archives Department has three, the
Bodleian Library has two
(MSS.Lyell Empt.33; Top.Derbys.b.1),
Lancashire RO has two in the Molyneux
muniments [NRA 0103], and Wigan RO has
two.
    Other Towneley family and estate papers
have been deposited by the 3rd Lord O'Hagan
in Lancashire RO at various dates since 1953
(*Guide to the Lancashire RO*, 1962, pp178-82.
NRA 1302) and by the Countess of Abingdon
in the Bodleian Library and the John Rylands
Library, Manchester University.

TOWNSHEND, Marquess
Raynham Hall, Norfolk. 1887
Eleventh R, 13-19 and App IV [19]

Sold with other Bacon and Townshend family papers at Sotheby's 10 Mar 1908 lot 121, 18 Dec 1911 (371 lots), 14 July 1924 lots 1-144 and at Hodgson's 3 July 1924 and 2 Apr 1925. For the dispersal of the Bacon papers see A Hassell Smith, *The papers of Nathaniel Bacon of Stiffkey* i, pp xx-xxxviii, Norfolk Record Society, 1978 and 1979.

Substantial groups including much material not noticed by the Report have been acquired by the British Library (Add MSS 37634-38, 38492-508, 41139-52, 41178K, 41305-08, 41654-56, 45733, 45902, 46856, 48981-82, 50006-12; Egerton MSS 3124-25; Add Ch 66712-13, 71290-97, and uncatalogued papers presented by TS Blakeney in 1977), the Bodleian Library (MSS.Eng.hist.c.194, d.117-18, 147-49, 211; Eng.lett.c.386), Norfolk RO (miscellaneous papers including items bought at Sotheby's 18 Dec 1911 lots 260-62 and 14 July 1924 lots 12, 26, 66, 72, 81, 88. Partially listed in NRA 4651, 15371).

Others are now in the Folger Library, Washington [NRA 20984], the Osborn Collection, Beinecke Library, Yale University [NRA 20037], the William L Clements Library, University of Michigan (*National union catalog* MSS 60-1275, 1334), the Public Archives of Canada (mainly in the Northcliffe collection) and the Library of Congress, Washington (Wilmington papers).

Some other family papers, not noticed by the Report, remain at Raynham Hall.

TRELAWNY, Sir John Salusbury Bt
Trelawne, West Looe, Cornwall. 1870
First R, x and App 50-53 [1]

The 13th cent French chronicle (p53) was sold at Sotheby's 28 June 1921, with four other MS books not noticed by the Report, and is now in the Pierpont Morgan Library, New York (M 751).

Some of the correspondence and personal papers (pp50-53) were also sold at Sotheby's 11 July 1921 lots 1-29. The present owners of the individual parts of these include the Duchy of Cornwall (lots 11, 24, 27, 28) and the Duke of Rutland (parts of lots 2, 3, 6, 13, through Captain CL Lindsay).

The deeds and rolls (p50) passed with the house to CC Morley in 1922 and were later given or sold to the British Museum (Add Ch 64002-888), Exeter City Library (*c*1650 deeds and court rolls now transferred to Devon RO), the Royal Institution of Cornwall, Truro, and the Revd WMM Picken.

The residue has remained untraced since the death as a resident at Puyvert, in France of Sir JW Salusbury-Trelawny Bt in 1944.

TRINITY HOUSE
1885
Eighth R, xiv and App I 235-62 [7]

The charter of incorporation of the Shipwrights' Company (p261) was restored to the Company in 1930. The grant of arms to the Corporation (p261) was destroyed by fire in 1940. The other material noticed remains at Trinity House.

TURNER, WH Esq
Turl Street, Oxford, until 1870
Second R, viii, xv and App 101-02 [1], 1871

The single item noticed remains in the Bodleian Library, Oxford (MS.Add.c.94).

UNDERWOOD, Charles Fleetwood Weston Esq
Somerby Hall, nr Barnetby, Lincs. 1885
Tenth R, 9-13 and App I 199-520 [10]

The twelve volumes of Edward Weston's papers noticed by the Report were sold at Sotheby's 15 Dec 1927 lot 916. Eight of these with fifteen further volumes were subsequently bought by WS Lewis in 1952 and 1958 and are now in the Lewis Walpole Library, Farmington, Connecticut [NRA 22339]. Vols VI and VII were bought by the British Museum in 1973 (Add MSS 57927-28; for other groups of Weston's correspondence acquired in 1971 and 1974 see also Add MSS 57305-08, 58213).

Further diplomatic and personal papers of Edward Weston remain in family possession [NRA 20870].

UNWIN, S Philip Esq
Bradford, Yorks. 1913, 1919
Eighteenth R, 101-02; Various collections VIII 569-92 [55]

Presented to the Brotherton Library, Leeds University, 1931 (MSS 8-10).

USHAW, College of St Cuthbert
1870
First R, xi and App 91-92 [1]

Remain in Ushaw College Library, Durham augmented by many later acquisitions [NRA 13674].

VERNEY, Sir Harry Bt
Claydon House, Bucks. 1879
Seventh R, xiv and App 433-509 [6]

Remain at Claydon House. Microfilm copies of the 17th-18th cent correspondence are held by the British Library (M/636(1)-(60)), the Library of Congress, Washington, the Beinecke Library, Yale University and Dartmouth College Library, Hanover,

New Hampshire. There are partial typescript lists of the deeds and the 19th-20th cent family papers [NRA 8849, 21959].

VERNON SMITH see Smith

VERULAM, Earl of
Gorhambury Park, Herts. 1906, 1907
Seventeenth R, 51-54; Verulam [64]

Deposited with other family papers in Hertfordshire RO at various dates since 1932 [NRA 7246], except the Somerset and Cornwall surveys (p184) and some of the 17th-18th cent correspondence (pp59-102; 114-77 passim).

VIDLER, JWC
Rye, Sussex. 1885
Tenth R, 14

The volume on shipbuilding by Edward Battine is now in the National Maritime Museum (SPB/28).

WALCOT, Revd John
Bitterley Court, Salop. 1885
Tenth R, 19 and App IV 418-20 [13]

Descended to JOH Walcot in Canada and were then dispersed, partly by auction at Sotheby's 8 Mar 1948 lots 671-76, when Nos 6, 7 and 22 were bought by another descendant, P Blencowe Esq.
  Other family and estate papers which descended to H Walcot and the Revd HJC Burton have been deposited in Shropshire RO at various dates since 1946 (*Guide to the Shropshire records*, 1952, pp116-19. NRA 16219). Some further papers have also been deposited there by solicitors at various dates since 1957 [NRA 11563].

WALLINGFORD, Corporation of
1877
Sixth R, App 572-95 [5]

Deposited in Berkshire RO at various dates since 1949 [NRA 3033].

WARWICK, RH Esq
Burgage Manor House, Southwell, Notts. 1890, 1891
Twelfth R, 46 and App IX 545-52 [27]

The commonplace book noticed by the Report was bought by the Duke of Westminster in 1895 as part of the JP Earwaker collection and presented by him to Chester Archaeological Society, which placed it in Chester City RO in 1969 [NRA 16683].

WATERFORD, Corporation of
1870, 1885
First R, App 131-32 [1]; Tenth R, 45 and App V 265-339 [14]

Remain in Waterford City Hall in the custody of the city manager.

WATERFORD, Marchioness of
Ford Castle, Northumberland. 1887, 1888
Eleventh R, 22-23 and App VII 58-81 [22]

The material noticed by the Report was included in the large collection of Delaval family papers from Seaton Delaval and Ford Castle presented to the Northumberland County History Committee in 1907 for use in the preparation of volumes viii and ix of the *History* and is summarily described by HHE Craster, *Proceedings of the Society of Antiquaries of Newcastle upon Tyne*, 3rd ser ii, 1905-06, pp36-41.
  The collection was subsequently divided. The eighty-five Stixwould Priory deeds (pp58-67), less No 11 which is missing, were given to the Bodleian Library 1920-24 [NRA 24249].
  The Waterford deeds listed pp67-76, the instructions to George Delaval 1707, 1710 (p76) and a letter from Samuel Foote (pp77-78) are among those given to Newcastle City Library in 1919 and subsequently transferred to Northumberland RO in 1963 and 1968 [NRA 10635].
  The rest of the letters noticed on pp76-81 and a good deal of other material not noticed by the Report cannot be accounted for.
See also: Delaval

WAUCHOPE, Andrew Esq
Niddrie, Midlothian. 1874
Fourth R, xxiii and App 537-38 [3]

In 1955 the items noticed were held by the family solicitors. Other family papers were bought by the National Library of Scotland in 1976 (Acc 6694) and 1977 (Acc 6993).

WEBB, Revd Thomas William
Hardwick Vicarage, Hereford. 1879
Seventh R, xv and App 681-93 [6]

Dispersed following the owner's death in 1885. Some of the material subsequently reappeared in sales at Sotheby's 4 Dec 1895 lots 556-601 passim (AC Ranyard sale), 6 July 1910 lots 189-90, and 22 Feb 1932 lot 2410 (Thorn Drury sale).
  The household account book (p691b), the memorandum book of Jeremiah Baines (p691a) and the letters and papers of Sarah Churchill, Duchess of Marlborough (p684) are now British Library Add MSS 32456, 32477, 38056.

The Rudhall and Brereton papers and Scudamore accounts (pp688-89, 692) are in Hereford City Library. The two volumes of Coningsby papers (p682) formerly in Hereford City Library are now in Hereford and Worcester RO, Hereford.

The volume of miscellaneous Pengelly papers (pp684-85) and the letters to Thomas Pengelly (p691b) are Bodleian Library MSS.Eng.lett.c.17, Add.c.267. The volume of surveys of royal lands in Cornwall 1649-53 is in the Duchy of Cornwall Office, London.

Other Pengelly and Scudamore family papers were presented to the British Museum by the Revd John Webb at various dates between 1830 and 1859 (Add MSS 6722-27, 11689, 11816, 19773-75, 22675).

WEBSTER, John Esq
Aberdeen. 1872
Third R, xxv and App 420-21 [2]
Dispersed by sale at Sotheby's 5 May 1892. The letters from the Earl of Seafield to Lord Godolphin 1703-08 were bought by the British Museum (Add MS 34180) which later also acquired the Danby correspondence 1678 at the Hodgkin sale in 1914 (Add MS 38849B). Seven letters have been identified in American repositories. Transcripts of the letters to Lord Godolphin on Scottish affairs 1703-05, given by Webster to Lord Stanhope, are among the Stanhope MSS in Kent AO.

WELBECK see Portland

WELLS, Bishop's Registry
1870
First R, App 92-93 [1]
Deposited in Somerset RO at various dates since 1959.

WELLS, Dean and Chapter of
1870-1919
First R, App 93-94 [1]; Third R, xix and App 351-64 [2]; Tenth R, 28-29 and App III [12]; Seventeenth R, 97-103; Eighteenth R, 197-201; Wells I, II [12]
Remain in the cathedral library.

WELLS, Vicars Choral of
1872
Third R, xix and App 364-65 [2]
Remain in the cathedral library.

WELLS, Corporation of
1870, 1872
First R, App 106-08 [1]; Third R, xix and App 350-51 [2]
Kept at Wells Town Hall in the custody of the town clerk.

WELLS, Bishop Bubwith's Almshouses
1881
Eighth R, App I 638-39 [7]
Kept at Wells Town Hall in the custody of the town clerk.

WELSH MSS see Banks; British Museum; Cardiff Free Library; Davies, DP Esq; Davies, JH Esq; Evans; Mostyn; Oxford, Jesus College; Panton; Reynolds; Williams, Sir John Bt; Williams, Revd R Peris; Wynne

WEMYSS, Randolph GE Esq
Wemyss Castle, Fife. 1872
Third R, xxv and App 422-23 [2]
Remain at Wemyss Castle. Not open for research.
See also: Rosslyn

WENLOCK, Corporation of
1885
Tenth R, 19 and App IV 420-24 [13]
Kept in the Corn Exchange, Wenlock in the custody of Much Wenlock Town Council. Access through the honorary archivist and curator of Wenlock Museum.

WENTWORTH, Mrs KM
Woolley Park, Yorks. 1903, 1904
Sixteenth R, 109-10; Various collections II 367-432 [55]
Deposited with other family papers in the Brotherton Library, Leeds University in 1946 and 1951 [NRA 15924], apart from eleven MSS placed on loan with some further papers in the library of the Yorkshire Archaeological Society, Leeds [NRA 12911]. The latter deposit originally also included cartularies of Pontefract and Monkbretton priories, not reported on, which were sold at Sotheby's 11 Apr 1961 and are now British Library Add MSS 50754-55.

WESTMINSTER, Dean and Chapter of
1870, 1874
First R, ix and App 94-97 [1]; Fourth R, xi-xii and App 171-99 [3]
Remain in Westminster Abbey Library. JA Robinson and MR James, *The MSS of Westminster Abbey*, Cambridge, 1909. Ker, *Medieval Libraries*, pp195-97, and *Medieval MSS* i, pp401-15.

WESTMINSTER, Catholic Archbishop of
1876
Fifth R, xii and App 470-76 [4]
The papers were rearranged and merged with other series of papers at Brompton Oratory

and later moved with these to the newly created Westminster Diocesan Archives in 1907. P Hughes, 'Westminster archives', *Dublin Review*, Oct 1937, pp300-10.

The Douai diaries and account and pension books (p476) were subsequently transferred to St Edmund's College, Ware [NRA 16303], but the account and pension books were brought back to Westminster with other college archives in 1973.

See also: London, Catholic Chapter of; Southwark; Stonyhurst College

WESTMINSTER, Marquess of

Eaton, Cheshire. 1872
Third R, xv and App 210-16 [2]

The Reading Abbey charters (p216) were given to the British Museum in 1873 (Add Ch 19571-659).

Thirty-six of the MS volumes (pp210-15) were sold with other material at Sotheby's 11 July 1966 lots 227-33, 19 July 1966 lots 471-511, 20 Feb 1967 lots 250-68. Immediate or eventual recipients of these include the British Library (journal of the Commissioners for Discoveries, p212b: Add MS 54198), the House of Lords Record Office (Order of passing Bills in Parliament, p214b), the Houghton Library, Harvard University (3), the Osborn Collection, Beinecke Library, Yale University (5), the Bancroft Library, University of California at Berkeley, and Princeton University Library.

The other fifteen MS volumes, mostly of family or Cheshire interest, and the deeds noticed on pp215-16, remain at the Eaton Estate Office with other family papers. Access through Cheshire RO. W Beaumont, *Calendar of ancient charters . . . preserved at Eaton Hall*, privately printed, 1862. Pott & Gardner, solicitors, *Schedule of deeds and documents in the muniment room at Eaton*, privately printed, 1896-98. Partial typescript list [NRA 13470].

Further family deeds and estate papers for Westminster, Buckinghamshire, Dorset, Gloucestershire and Hertfordshire from the Grosvenor Estate Office in London were deposited in Westminster City Libraries in 1979. Some papers of Sibell, Lady Grosvenor remain at the Grosvenor Estate Office but are not generally open for research.

WESTMORLAND, Earl of

Apethorpe, Northants. 1885
Tenth R, 2-4 and App IV 1-59 [13]

Most of the material noticed by the Report was sold with other family papers at Sotheby's 13 July 1887 (65 lots), Christie's 16 July 1892 lots 411-62 passim, or Puttick and Simpson's 27 July 1893 lots 243-620 passim. Some lots, however, from the 1892 sale were bought in and are now either among the family papers

deposited by the 14th and 15th Earls of Westmorland in Northamptonshire RO (A, B, F, G, I, and the account books on p58) or among those deposited by Captain HWN Fane in Lincolnshire AO (E) [NRA 10303].

Eventual recipients of material sold include the British Library (Add MSS 34213-23, 34251), Cambridge University Library (Add 3020-21, 3114-19, 3851, 4082, 4189), London University Library (the letters from C Billingsley, p34), the Houghton Library, Harvard University (the Fugitive poetry, pp44-47: fMS Eng 645), the Folger Library, Washington (A short view of K Henrie the 3, p58) and the Huntington Library, San Marino (the 6th Earl's letter book 1705-08, p58).

Other family and estate papers are among the Dashwood family papers in the Bodleian Library (MS.D.D.Dashwood (Bucks). NRA 0892) and among the Stapleton family papers in Berkshire RO and Kent AO [NRA 1241, 7749].

The papers of the 10th Earl of Westmorland as Lord Lieutenant of Ireland were presented to the State Paper Office, Dublin in 1883 [NRA 22312]. The diplomatic correspondence and papers of the 11th Earl of Westmorland were sold at Sotheby's 1 Aug 1950 (British Library microfilm M/509-29). The correspondence of Priscilla, Countess of Westmorland and other family papers that descended to Miss Rachel Weigall were sold at Sotheby's 2 Mar 1965 lots 452-67 or deposited in Kent AO in 1968 [NRA 15266].

WESTON UNDERWOOD see Underwood

WEYMOUTH AND MELCOMBE REGIS, Corporation of

1876
Fifth R, xix and App 575-76 [4]

In the custody of Weymouth and Portland Borough Council. Access through the curator, Weymouth Museum. HJ Moule, *Descriptive catalogue of the charters, minute books and other documents of the borough of Weymouth and Melcombe Regis, 1252-1800*, Weymouth, 1883.

Other 19th-20th cent borough records were deposited in Dorset RO in 1971.

See also: Sherren

WHARNCLIFFE, Earl of

Wortley Hall, Yorks, Belmont, Perthshire, and Dundee. 1872-76
Third R, xvi and App 224-26 [2]; Fourth R, xxiii and App 518 [3]; Fifth R, xx and App 621-23 [4]

Almost all the charters from Belmont and Dundee were sold at Sotheby's 9 June 1920 lots 76-96. Some Scottish estate papers were destroyed at Wortley Hall during the Second World War. The Wortley Hall papers were deposited in Sheffield Central Library with other family and estate papers in 1951 [NRA 1077].

A few deeds and estate papers 17th-20th cent are held by Messrs T & JW Barty, Dunblane [NRA 14867].

WHITGREAVE, Francis Esq
Burton Manor, Staffs. 1870
First R, xi and App 61-62 [1]

The Relation of the Journey of twelve English Students 1622 was given to Stonyhurst College, Lancs in 1923 (MS E.III.1). The volume of poems of Sir Aston Cockayne was sold at Sotheby's 30 Jan 1956 lot 417 and is now MS b275 in the Osborn Collection, Beinecke Library, Yale University.

Of papers not noticed by the Report, three MSS were sold at Sotheby's 16 July 1928 lot 581, some deeds were given to the William Salt Library, Stafford in 1949 [NRA 6769] and further family papers have been deposited in Staffordshire RO at various dates since 1957 [NRA 9417].

WILBRAHAM, George F Esq
Delamere House, Cheshire. 1872, 1874
Third R, xvii and App 292-93 [2]; Fourth R, xv and App 416-17 [3]

Mostly sold at Sotheby's 20 June 1898 lots 86, 118, 239, 482, 622, 19 Mar 1928 lots 60, 236, 240, 20 July 1959 lots 401, 414-16, 28 Mar 1960 lot 126 and in other unidentified sales. The Account of another Journey into France is now Bodleian Library MS.Eng.misc.e.234. The 15th cent Latin and English vocabulary is Bristol University Library DM 14. Wycliffe's translations of the Psalms and of the Gospels are John Rylands Library, Manchester University Eng MS 88 and Cambridge University Library Add 6684 respectively. Some family diaries and four account books including that of Richard and Thomas Minshull were bought by Sir Randle Baker Wilbraham and remain at Rode Hall.

The Wilbraham remembrances (Third R, p292) was deposited in 1964 in Cheshire RO, which also holds other groups of family papers [NRA 7063, 9848].

WILLES, Mrs EW
Goodrest, Berks. 1871, 1872
Second R, xxi and App 103 [1]; Third R, xxvi and App 435 [2]

The three volumes relating to Chief Baron Willes [NRA 23547] were withdrawn by Mrs AE Willes from Warwickshire RO in 1979. Microfilm copies of the second and third volumes and of some related material are held by the Public Record Office of Northern Ireland and by

Warwickshire RO. The latter also bought some Willes of Newbold Comyn estate papers in 1979.

WILLIAMS, Dr, Library of
1872
Third R, xxi and App 365-68 [2]
Remain at the library [NRA 13168].

WILLIAMS, Sir John Bt
Plas Llan Stephan, Carmarthens. 1903, 1904
Sixteenth R, 134; Welsh MSS II ii 420-782 [48]

Given by Sir John Williams to the National Library of Wales between 1909 and 1916.

Other MSS acquired by the Library from this source are listed in *Additional MSS in the collections of Sir John Williams Bt, 1921* (MSS 1-446), National Library of Wales *Handlist* I, 1943 (MSS 447-500) and III, 1961 (MSS 8086-8101) and *Calendar of Wynn (of Gwydir) papers 1515-1690*, 1926.

WILLIAMS, Revd R Peris
Wrexham Rectory, Denbighs. 1902, 1904
Sixteenth R, 134; Welsh MSS II i 346-66 [48]

The three Havod MSS were sold to the National Library of Wales in 1914 (MSS 872-74).

WILSON, Matthew Esq
Eshton Hall, Yorks. 1872
Third R, xviii and App 293-300 [2]

The forty-one volumes of John Hopkinson's antiquarian papers were sold at Sotheby's 31 May 1916 lot 337 and are now in Bradford Archives Department.

Estate papers from Eshton Hall and some West Riding quarter sessions account books 1810-18 were sold to the Brotherton Library, Leeds University in 1976 [NRA 21696]. Some further small groups of deeds and estate papers were deposited in Leeds Archives Department by solicitors in 1966 [NRA 12935] and in Lancashire RO in 1976.

WILTON see Pembroke

WILTSHIRE, Records of the Quarter Sessions of
1901, 1904
Sixteenth R, 95-96; Various collections I 65-176 [55]

In Wiltshire RO. *Guide to the records in the custody of the clerk of the peace for Wiltshire*, 1959.

WINCHESTER, Corporation of
1877
Sixth R, App 595-605 [5]

In Hampshire RO. *Winchester city archives, general catalogue*, 1962.

WINCHILSEA AND NOTTINGHAM, Earl of
1870
First R, viii-ix and App 14-34 [1]

Most of the Hatton charters and correspondence noticed on pp viii-ix and 14-30 were sold to the British Museum in 1873 (Add MSS 29548-96; Add Ch 19788-22613). Most of the remaining books, papers etc (pp30-34) are with the family papers deposited with Northamptonshire Record Society in 1930 and now in Northamptonshire RO [NRA 4485]. ES Scroggs, *Catalogue of the Finch-Hatton MSS*, typescript, 1931.

A forged 12th cent Westminster Abbey charter, not noticed by the Report, was sold at Sotheby's 19 June 1979 lot 35 and returned to the Abbey in 1980.

See also: Finch

WINDSOR, Dean and Chapter of St George's Chapel
1914, 1919
Eighteenth R, 204-06; Various collections VII 10-43 [55]

Remain at the Aerary, St George's Chapel, Windsor in the care of the archivist. JN Dalton, *The MSS of St George's Chapel, Windsor Castle*, Windsor, 1957 [NRA 18513].

WINDSOR CASTLE see Stuart MSS

WINNINGTON, Sir Thomas Bt
Stanford Court, Worcs. 1870
First R, x and App 53-55 [1]

Most of the papers noticed were destroyed in a fire at Stanford Court in 1882. A few MSS were sold at Hodgson's 25 May 1932 lots 461-81 passim and at Sotheby's 17 Dec 1945 lot 545. Of these, the 'new Book of Rents, Annuities' (p536) is now British Library Egerton MS 3054. Thomas Dineley's History from Marble is Bodleian Library MS.Top.Gen.d.19. Four MSS are in American libraries.

A group of Worcestershire title deeds and a few family papers were bought by Birmingham Reference Library in 1945. Other family and estate papers were deposited by solicitors in Hereford and Worcester RO, Worcester in 1970 [NRA 14331].

WISBECH, Corporation of
1883
Ninth R, xiv-xv and App I 293-99 [8]

In Wisbech and Fenland Museum, Wisbech.

WITHAM, Mrs Dorothy Mary Maxwell
Kirkconnell, Kirkcudbrightshire. 1876
Fifth R, xx-xxi and App 650-54 [4]

Remain at Kirkconnell House [NRA 10440] apart from the letters from 'Royal and Noble Personages' (pp650-52) reported missing in 1947.

WODEHOUSE, Edmond R Esq
1892
Thirteenth R, 48-50 and App IV 405-94 [31]

Presented to the British Museum, 1915 (Add MSS 39218-52; Add Ch 59797-61129).

WOMBWELL, Sir George Bt
Newburgh Priory, Yorks. 1903, 1904
Sixteenth R, 103-05; Various collections II 1-226 [55]

Most of the documents listed were deposited in North Yorkshire RO in 1967. Two MSS were sold with the library at Sotheby's 14 Apr 1924 including the Vita Sanctorum (pp24-27), acquired by Cardiff Central Library.

Some other family papers were sold privately in 1924. A letter book 1665-85 and notebook of the 1st Earl of Fauconberg are now British Library Add MSS 41254-55. Some account books and rentals are in the Houghton Library, Harvard University (MSS Eng 603F-605F) and in Columbia University Libraries, New York (Montgomery collection).

WOOD, Hon (Edward) Frederick Lindley, 1st Earl of Halifax
Temple Newsam, Yorks. 1913, 1919
Eighteenth R, 89-94; Various collections VIII 1-195 [55]

Mostly among the Ingram family and estate papers which were sold to Leeds Corporation in 1937 and are now in Leeds Archives Department [Partial list NRA 7398]. Some thirty documents, mainly autograph letters, were sold separately with other papers from Temple Newsam at Sotheby's 8 June 1936 lots 169-255.

The 1st Earl's own family, personal and official papers from Hickleton and Garrowby were deposited in the Borthwick Institute of Historical Research, York in 1980 [NRA 8128].

WOODCHESTER, Dominican Priory
1871
Second R, xiii and App 146-49 [1]

Most of the eighteen MSS listed by the
Report are now with the archives of the
English Dominican province. Access through
the archivist, St Dominic's Priory, New Bridge
Street, Newcastle upon Tyne.

WOODFORDE, Revd AJ
Ansford, Somerset. 1884
Ninth R, xviii and App II 496-99 [8]

Sold to New College, Oxford in 1970 as part of
a collection of 108 books and papers relating
to the family. FW Steer, *Archives of
New College, Oxford*, 1974, pp112-21.
   Some other family papers were deposited in
Somerset RO in 1956. Further papers have
been deposited in or sold to the Bodleian
Library, Oxford at various dates between 1959
and 1976 [NRA 18992].

WORCESTER, Bishop's Registry
1895, 1896
Fourteenth R, 45 and App VIII 204-05 [37]

Deposited in Hereford and Worcester RO,
Worcester at various dates since 1956
[NRA 8204].

WORCESTER, Dean and Chapter of
1895, 1896
Fourteenth R, 44-45 and App VIII
165-203 [37]

Most of the items noticed remain in the
cathedral library [NRA 21008] with some
additional MSS [NRA 17107]. The Complaints
against Sir John Bourne (p184) is apparently
missing. The visitation book 1540 (p183) was
deposited in Hereford and Worcester RO,
Worcester which also holds the manorial and
estate records [NRA 7450] and microfilm
copies of many other capitular records.

WORCESTER, County of
1901, 1904
Sixteenth R, 100-01; Various collections
I 282-326 [55]

In Hereford and Worcester RO, Worcester.

WORCESTER, St Andrew's Church
1881
Eighth R, App I 638 [7]

The five deeds noticed have not been traced.
They are not among the parish records
deposited in Hereford and Worcester RO,
Worcester.

WREST PARK see Cowper, Countess

WREXHAM see Williams, Revd R Peris

WROTTESLEY, Lord
Wrottesley, Staffs. 1871
Second R, x and App 46-49 [1]

Destroyed in a fire, 1897. The extracts
published by G Wrottesley, 'History of the
family of Wrottesley, co Stafford', *Genealogist*,
new ser xv-xix, were reprinted in William Salt
Archaeological Society *Collections for a history
of Staffordshire*, new ser vi, pt ii, 1903.

WYKEHAM MARTIN, Cornwallis Esq
The Hill, Purton, Wilts. 1909, 1919
Eighteenth R, 127-35; Various collections VI,
xxix-xliv 297-434 [55]

Sold in 1932 and 1934 to the National
Maritime Museum (COR/1-56) which bought
further papers of Admiral Cornwallis at the
Harmsworth sale, Sotheby's 24 May 1948
lots 4702-19 passim.

WYKEHAM MARTIN, Philip Esq
Leeds Castle, Kent. 1877
Sixth R, xiv and App 465-68 [5]

The ten letters from Archbishop Wake to
David Wilkins, most of the papers relating to
Gibraltar 1762-82 and a few other items also
noted on pp467-68 were included in a small
group of family and estate papers presented to
Kent AO in 1938 [NRA 5455]. Sir Peter
Thompson's copy of Short Memorials
was sold to the Osborn Collection, Beinecke
Library, Yale University in 1954. The
commonplace book of Brian Fairfax containing
Iter Boreale was bought by Edinburgh
University Library in 1958 (MS DK.5.25).
   Some estate maps and MSS, including
another copy of Short Memorials and
Alexander Smyth's diary (p466) were sold with
the Leeds Castle library at Gorringe's, Lewes,
Sussex 13 Dec 1960 lots 472-85.
   The remaining MSS noticed by the Report
have not been located since 1927 when they
were placed in store following the sale of
Leeds Castle. Some may be among the
Fairfax MSS bought privately by the
12th Baron Fairfax of Cameron but not open
for research. A copy of JA Symington's
typescript catalogue of this collection is held by
Berkshire RO.
   For the Fairfax correspondence (pp xiv, 465)
see WJ Connor 'The Fairfax archives: a study
in dispersal', *Archives*, xi, 1973, pp76-85.
Some of the letters were resold with other
Civil War papers at Sotheby's 21 July 1980
lots 36, 41 and bought by the Leeds Castle
Trustees.

WYNNE family
Peniarth, Merioneths. 1870-1904
Second R, xii and App 103-06 (WWE Wynne)
[1]; Fifteenth R, 47-49; Sixteenth R, 133;
Welsh MSS I ii, iii (WRM Wynne) [48]

The Hengwrt-Peniarth MSS were bought by
Sir John Williams Bt for the National Library
of Wales on its foundation in 1909. *Handlist*,
I, 1943, pp iii-xxiii, 1-22. Further family
papers were bought by the Library in 1981.

YAXLEY, Parish of
1885
Tenth R, 26 and App IV 463-66 [13]

Deposited with other parish records in
Suffolk RO, Ipswich, 1971 [NRA Suffolk
parish reports].

YELVERTON see Calthorpe

YORK, Dean and Chapter of
1870
First R, App 97 [1]

Remain in York Minster Library. Ker,
Medieval Libraries, pp216-17. The probate and
peculiar records of the dean and chapter, not
noticed by the Report, have been deposited in
the Borthwick Institute of Historical Research,
York. *Guide to the archive collections in the
Borthwick Institute*, 1973. [NRA 20282].

YORK, Corporation of
1870
First R, App 108-10 [1]

In York City Archives [NRA 7142]. W Giles,
*Catalogue of the charters, house books etc
belonging to the corporation of York*, York,
1908. RJ Green, *York City Archives*, 1971.

**YORK,
Company of Merchant Adventurers of**
1870
First R, App 110 [1]

Remain at the Merchant Adventurers' Hall,
Fossgate, York [NRA 12593].

**YORKSHIRE, Lord Lieutenant and
Justices of the Peace of the North Riding
of**
1883
Ninth R, xvi and App I 329-49 [8]

Now in North Yorkshire RO.

YORKSHIRE, West Riding of
1883
Ninth R, xvi and App I 324-29 [8]

Now in West Yorkshire RO.

**YORKSHIRE PHILOSOPHICAL
SOCIETY**
1870
First R, App 110 [1]

The two items noticed by the Report, viz the
compotus of St Mary's Abbey York 1528-29
and the manumission *c*1220, have not been
traced.
    Other papers, including those of
Eustace Strickland, were transferred to
York City Archives in 1966 [NRA 16393].
Twenty deeds 13th-19th cent were deposited
in Leeds Archives Department in 1969
[NRA 19414].

ZETLAND, Earl of
Arlington Street, London SW. 1870
First R, xi and App 44 [1]

Deposited in North Yorkshire RO with other
Dundas family and estate papers [NRA 16269].
    The papers of the 2nd Marquess of Zetland,
not noticed by the Report, were deposited in
the India Office Library and Records in 1961
(MSS Eur D 609. NRA 20539). Kerse estate
papers have been deposited in the Scottish
Record Office (GD 173, 236. NRA 10745) and
some Earldom of Orkney estate papers in
Orkney AO [NRA 15343].

Other collections examined

The following collections were also reported to have been examined
but no details of their contents were published:

AGNEW, Robert Vans Esq
Barnbarroch, Wigtownshire. 1872
Third R, x and App 402 [2]

Family muniments. Now in the Scottish
Record Office (GD 99).

BLANTYRE, Lord
Lennoxlove, E Lothian. 1872
Third R, x, xxii and App 402 [2]

Family muniments. Remain with the Duke of
Hamilton at Lennoxlove [NRA 10979].

FLETCHER, Andrew Esq
Saltoun Hall, E Lothian. 1872
Third R, x, xxii and App 402 [2]

Family muniments. Now in the National
Library of Scotland [NRA 10147].

**HAMILTON, JGC Esq,
1st Baron Hamilton**
Dalzell, Lanarkshire. 1872
Third R, App 402 [2]

Family muniments. Bequeathed to
Motherwell Public Library in 1952
[NRA 10162].

HEBER PERCY, Algernon Charles Esq
Hodnet, Salop. 1885
Tenth R, App IV 378 [13]

'Title deeds and papers of no historical
interest'. Thought to remain in family
possession.

KYNASTON, Revd WCE
Hardwick, Ellesmere, Salop. 1885
Tenth R, App IV 378 [13]

'Title deeds and papers of no historical
interest'. Some family estate accounts and
other papers have been deposited in
Shropshire RO.

LENNOX, Hon Mrs Hanbury
Lennox Castle, Stirlingshire. 1872
Third R, x and App 402 [2]

Family muniments. Remain at the Lennox
Estate Office, Campsie Glen by Glasgow.

PETERSFIELD, Corporation of
1885
Tenth R, 23

The 'scanty' records (27 documents) are now
deposited in Hampshire RO.

**SCRYMGEOUR WEDDERBURN, HJ Esq,
de jure 11th Earl of Dundee**
1926
Nineteenth R, 7

The typescript report that was ready for press
in 1920 (45pp) calendared letters and papers of
David Scrymgeour as sheriff depute for
Inverness 1748-68.
  Some of the family papers remain at Birkhill
[NRA 10549]. Others have been deposited in
the Scottish Record Office (GD 137).

TEMPEST, Mrs
Dalguise House, Dunkeld, Perthshire. 1926
Nineteenth R, 7

The typescript report (350pp) that was ready
for press in 1920 has not been traced. The
papers are now in the Scottish Record Office
(GD 38). *Gifts and Deposits* i, pp83-87.

**WOLRYCHE WHITMORE, Revd
Francis Henry**
Dudmaston Hall, Quatt, Salop. 1885
Tenth R, App IV 378 [13]

The title deeds and papers referred to were
listed by the Commission at Dudmaston in
1953 [NRA 4482] and deposited in
Shropshire Record Office by Lady Labouchere
in 1973.

Printed in England for Her Majesty's Stationery Office by Albert Gait Ltd., Grimsby
Dd   699049   C30